# ABOVE LONDON

PHOTOGRAPHY BY ROBERT CAMERON
TEXT BY ALISTAIR COOKE

PUBLISHED BY
CAMERON AND COMPANY
SAN FRANCISCO, CALIFORNIA

# CAMERON AND COMPANY

543 Howard Street   San Francisco, California 94105   415/777-5582

First Printing, 1980
Second Printing, 1981
Third Printing, 1983
Fourth Printing, 1986
Fifth Printing, 1989
Sixth Printing, 1992
Seventh Printing, 1993

Library of Congress Catalog Card Number 80-80944
Above London ISBN 0-918684-10-2

Book design by
**JANE OLAUG KRISTIANSEN**

Color film processing by John Piercy Limited, London
Typography by Reeder Type, Inc., Fremont, California
Color separation and printing by Dai Nippon Printing Co., Hong Kong

# THE BIRD'S—EYE VIEW
## by ALISTAIR COOKE

It is, I suppose, only since the Second World War that great numbers of ordinary people have seen the world from the air and come to share Saint-Exupéry's lyrical view of rolling snowfields of cloud, the shafting light on forests and vast expanses of farmland, the doll-like charm of towns seen as miniatures of the human community. On the other hand, Evelyn Waugh once remarked that "the aerial view of anything degrades everything it encloses." Between these extremes, but inclining more to the poet than the cynic, is the view that Bob Cameron (the photographer), Andrew von Preussen (our pilot), and I chose to express in filming, from a helicopter, a great metropolis.

Once the thing was done, it was obvious to the viewer-reader (though it was not always obvious to us in the doing) that the bird's-eye view triumphantly vindicates Saint-Exupéry but sometimes has a hard time discrediting Waugh. Even though we made a point of filming some of the London squares in the early spring, before the foliage had blanketed the facades of the houses, we reluctantly concluded that domestic architecture—in which Englishmen have shown a special genius (especially through the 18th and early 19th centuries)—is not seen at its best from the Civil Aviation Authority's compulsory minimum height of 1,000 ft. above the rooftops of the central city: the camera frame compresses too dense and wide a field of vision.

But, luckily, the regulations are more liberal over the river (500 ft. for a one-engine helicopter that is allowed to tilt and hold a stable position) and the river is the great lifeline of London as of no other metropolis I can think of. Rome has its Tiber, Paris its Seine, New Orleans its Mississippi, but London is laid out along the whole length of the river and it was a maritime capital before anything else. Fortunately, therefore, the great public buildings, cathedrals, law courts, fortresses, royal mansions and country houses were close by the river. Hence, we decided that the bird's-eye view could offer a unique panorama, at once lyrical and documentary, if we approached the city from the river and followed it—with occasional swooping detours to the north and south—from its estuary to its near-vanishing point as a pleasure stream running through placid meadows to a country horizon.

As for the rest of the city, even over its densest concentrations of brick and stone, one who has known London for over fifty years was excited to see it anew and re-discover the great variety of its life, landscape and frozen history from an angle that is denied to the earth-bound sightseer. The advantages of this aerial reconnaissance to the tourist will, I hope, be plain. He will know at a glance where he is, what he's near, and what unsuspected jewels lie round the corner, or half a mile away from any chosen target. We can say without mock modesty that we do not know another book on London quite like this: the capital city became a new found land that surprised us, and we hope it will equally surprise and delight both the newcomer and the oldest inhabitant.

# LONDON—ANCIENT AND MODERN

We can only dimly imagine what a Roman map of LONDINIUM would look like, but thanks to the grinding diligence of some German cartographer (visitor?) we have here a vivid map of the London of the late 16th century. It was engraved by Braun and Hogenberg and published in the German *Civitates Orbis Terrarum* in 1574, when Shakespeare was 10. Only two copper plates of the original remain, one of which is in the Museum of London.

From the earliest times, this was the most crowded part of the city, indeed the city itself, since the Romans built only one bridge across the river (where London Bridge now is). It was therefore the only link between the north bank (HOLBORN AND THE CITY, as we know them today) and the south bank town of SOUTHWARK, on which all roads from the south and the southeast converged.

In its heyday, at the beginning of the 17th century, Southwark was the center of things, as dense in a miniature way as it is today. Here were the churches, the fairs, the playhouses, the brothels, scores of inns, and prisons (of which The Clink, long gone, has left us its name.)

In the center is the long thin spire of the old St. Paul's, a Gothic church dedicated to St. Paul. In the left-hand corner can be plainly seen Lambeth Palace, the London home of the archbishops of Canterbury, which had been standing for almost four centuries when this map was drawn. In the righthand corner, across the river from a "Beere House" is the Tower of London.

(OPPOSITE) The same view today, as plainly as we could shoot it. Cannon Street railway bridge is in the middle, between Southwark Bridge (left) and London Bridge (right), at the southern end of which the ancient Southwark Cathedral is snuggled, or imprisoned, inside a noose of train tracks. (As it is drawn, in the same place, on the map). The vivid white building in the center is a tele-communications headquarters.

The House att Chelsey in the County of Middlesex one of the Seats of the Most Noble & Potent Prince Henry Duke of Beaufort Marquesse & Earle of Worcester Baron Herbert of Chepstow Raglan & Gower and Knight of the Most Noble order of the Garter.

L. Knyff D.

I. Kip Sca.

This engraving was done in 1708, when CHELSEA was practically the personal domain of the Duke of Beaufort, whose house (facing the lawn with a circular walk, and a carriageway down to the river) was built on the site of the mansion of Chelsea's most famous resident: Sir Thomas More. The western end of the house abuts on what is now Beaufort Street, which runs straight on to Battersea Bridge. (OPPOSITE) In both pictures, Cheyne Walk can be clearly seen starting just west of the bridge.

Beaufort's estate bordered that of the Earl of Ranelagh, who turned his lands into a famous pleasure garden. It must have been a delectable place to roam around in. Jonathan Swift thought so in 1711, though—in a prevision of the Chelsea hippie-swingers of the 1960s—he found it marred by "a mighty increase of dirty wenches in straw hats."

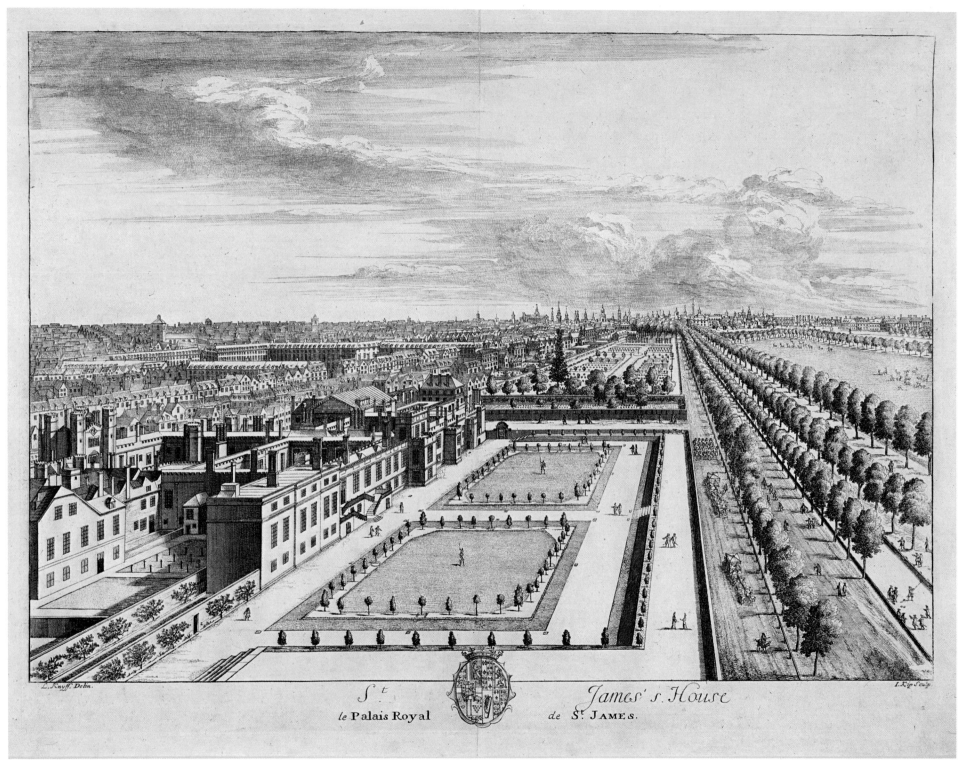

L. Knyff Delin.

Sᵗ             *James's House*

*le* **Palais Royal**        *de* Sᵗ. **JAMES.**

I. Kip Sculp.

This French bird's-eye view of ST. JAMES'S was drawn in 1708, just ten years after Whitehall was burned down and the royal family had retreated to these state apartments (designed by Wren for Charles the Second) and made them the official London residence of the sovereign. (To this day, this is the theoretical center of the Court, and all ambassadors are accredited "to the Court of St. James's"). Queen Anne and George the Fourth were born here, and the monarchs through the Hanoverians lived here until Queen Victoria established a precedent and moved into Buckingham Palace.

The first palace was built by Henry the Eighth on the site of a lepers' hospital. About all that is left of it is the Tudor gate-tower that faces St. James's Street and can be seen in both pictures (OPPOSITE) on the left edge at about 8 o'clock.

The most interesting discrepancy between the two views is at the far end of THE MALL where, in 1708, the tree-lined avenue (which was a boulevard adjoining a riding path) turns left to end at Carlton House Terrace. This left-angled extension was abolished when Admiralty Arch was erected in 1910 to provide a direct entrance to Trafalgar Square and, for the first time, to turn the Mall into one of the finest processional avenues in Europe.

This bird's-eye view west from what is now Tower Bridge was printed in 1770. The perspective in both pictures is much the same and so are the relative positions of ST. PAUL'S and THE MONUMENT (which–after Wren's design–went up in 1677 to commemorate the Great Fire of London that eleven years earlier had destroyed 89 churches–including the original St. Paul's–460 streets and 13,000 houses).

In the 1770 version, the Monument is greatly distorted to match the height of St. Paul's; in ours (OPPOSITE), it is almost buried in the surrounding steel and concrete (it is in a line directly below the right edge of the dome of St. Paul's).

In the latter half of the 19th century, there was a lively scientific to-do about the use of balloons

a. for making meteorological observations and
b. for seeing how high you could go without becoming asphyxiated.

In 1875, four Frenchmen proved the second point dramatically by getting up to 28,000 feet, from which height only one of them came back alive. History does not record how long in 1886 two intrepid English draftsmen, W. L. Wyllie and H. W. Brewer, stayed up just to the west of Westminster Abbey to draw, in such exact detail, this view of a great part of the city. It is unlikely, anyway, that the puffs and swirls of bituminous smoke were put in later as touches of artistic license. In the 1880's, London luxuriated in its smog—before the word had been invented—as a sign of the energy and prosperity of the world's first port and the capital of Empire.

(OPPOSITE) We reproduced the angle of the Wyllie and Brewer shot to show the growth of the city on the south bank and also to reveal the new clarity of light and atmosphere that Londoners enjoy since the carrying out of the Clean Air Act of 1956. Ironically, the picture was taken on a warm summer's day when the Wyllie-Brewer effect was unwittingly reproduced, not by industrial smog but by heat haze.

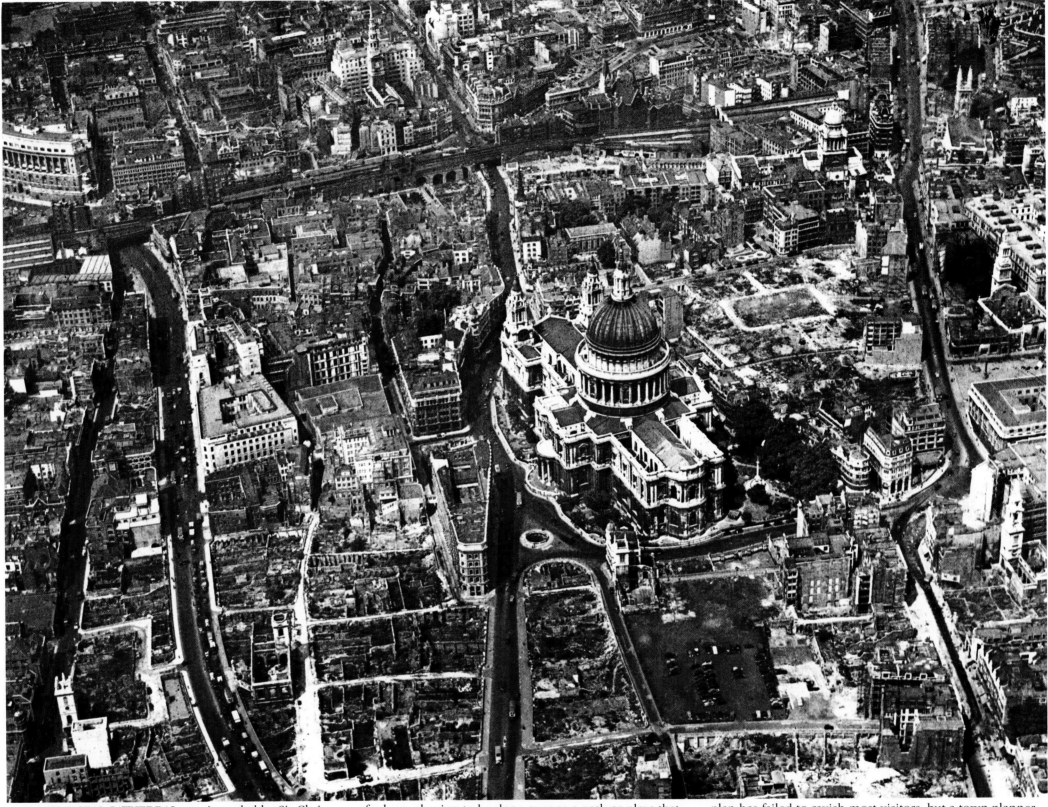

ST. PAUL'S CATHEDRAL was intended by Sir Christopher Wren to be the central jewel of a baroque park. The greed of the merchants and the high price of land defeated him. By the Second World War, it was just one tall tree in a jungle of brick and stone. During the Blitz, the nightly courage of the firewardens saved St. Paul's from destruction. Here, we can see how the widespread havoc of the Nazi bombs offered once again the prospect of a large clearing to be done over as a park or plaza that could set off the glory of the cathedral.

(OPPOSITE) But once again the same mercantile pressures were applied to strangle this dream. Not before, however, Sir William Holford had successfully proposed to enclose the Cathedral with "a succession of open and block vistas, similar to those in a mediaeval town." The plan has failed to ravish most visitors, but a town-planner no less distinguished than Lewis Mumford finds it full of "functional suppleness and aesthetic variety, well-filled spaces and friendly enclosures," very different from "the deadly uniformity, the visual bleakness (and) the inhuman scale of the grandiose city plans that Le Corbusier put forward from the 1920s on." Here, anyway, is how it looks today.

# BY RIVER INTO THE CITY

From its wide tidal mouth on the North Sea, The Thames flows past long sand flats and such ancient shore points as The Knock, Grain Spit, Deadman's Point, Mucking Flats and Coalhouse Point and narrows in Gravesend Reach to TILBURY.

Here, about 25 miles up the estuary, the river comes to life as a commercial waterway, and we know we are approaching a great city port.

TILBURY DOCKS, looking south and east. The original dock and its three branches are at the upper left. The great extension dock, cutting through the middle, divides off the forest products terminals (left) from the container terminals and berths (right) and a huge grain terminal.

(OPPOSITE) Fifteen miles farther west is WOOLWICH, which has the only free ferry on the Thames. It was started in 1889 and links the north and south ends of the Circular Roads.

(OPPOSITE) When it is finished in 1981 or 82, THE THAMES BARRIER, a radical flood control device, will be the biggest movable barrier in the world.

In 1953, the year of Elizabeth the Second's coronation, a flood in the Thames estuary drowned 300 people. It was only the most dramatic warning of a growing peril to the city itself. London is sinking on its clay bed, and the tide levels are gradually rising. The Thames is also subject to what meteorologists know as "surge tides." For many years, the risk of floods has been met by raising the river's banks. But in 1971, the Greater London Council concluded that the building of higher and higher dikes was no solution to the central and menacing problem: the whole of southeast England is sinking at what geologists regard as an alarming rate.

The Thames Barrier, decided on after various alternatives were debated, is the answer. It is a sunken sectorgate barrier with four 200-foot openings, two 100-foot openings, and four smaller openings for light vessels. Instead of drop gates, which would have required massive superstructures, the system is rooted in gates planted in casings on the comparatively stable bed of Woolwich Reach. The gates are on pivots and can be swung up separately in fifteen minutes. In a surge tide or other critical situation, the whole barrier can be elevated.

(RIGHT) The flood barrier under construction at night.

Just west of the Barrier on the south bank, a riverside wharf and a CONTAINER SHIP ready for loading.

(OPPOSITE) Almost due north from the busiest part of the river is the LEA VALLEY, historically the source of London's water supply. It is being developed as a protected recreation area. Here, close by Epping Forest, is a reservoir and trout-breeding ground that provides the city with its biggest heron and cormorant sanctuary.

In the late afternoon, the poplar-lined fairways of this golf course, near Epping Forest, look less like London and more like the romantic backdrop to an Italian Renaissance portrait.

Still within the eastern waterworks system is the Everyman suburb of CHINGFORD, squeaky clean and a home gardener's paradise. The central street, as straight as a Roman road, is Myddelton Avenue, named after Sir Hugh Myddelton who, in 1613 devised London's first water supply system. Running parallel with the fringe of greensward is a flood relief channel.

(OPPOSITE) HACKNEY MARSH, closer to the river and on the northeastern edge of Greater London (or, rather, what the Civil Aviation Authority defines as "The Specified Area", i.e. the densest part of the city) is an astonishing oasis of greenery in the encroaching suburbs: a 940-acre piece of grassland. It provides more lavishly than any other part of the United Kingdom for the practice of a single sport. No less than 110 soccer pitches.

On a fine Saturday afternoon in the spring or autumn, it presents a spectacle to blow the mind of the most rabid soccer fan: seen from the air, 2,420 midgets simultaneously playing the national winter game.

(OPPOSITE) What is now THE ROYAL NAVAL COLLEGE, on the south bank of the Thames at GREENWICH, took almost a century, on and off, to complete in the form that we see it. It started as a little house for James The First's queen, in 1618. After the Civil War, Charles I commissioned a royal palace (lower right). The rest of it was finished in 1705 and converted into a hospital for old seamen. However, by a mid-19th century act of parliament, its 2700 boarders were liberally pensioned off and moved, since then it has been the headquarters of students at The Royal Naval College.

This splendid harmony of 17th Century building is a combined tribute to three architectural geniuses. To Palladio, who inspired it. To Inigo Jones, who began it. And to Sir Christopher Wren, who finished it.

Andrea Palladio was the 16th century Italian who revolutionized the cities of Italy with his revived classical designs. Shortly after his death, a young English architect, Inigo Jones visited Italy and became a fervent disciple of Palladio's innovations. Being commissioned to build "the Queen's House" (top center), he produced this original which, with its Ionic center and plain flanking wings, must have been a shocker to Londoners, surrounded still by Tudor gables and heavy, if picturesque, Jacobean. To Americans, it looks like a little White House, designed—astonishingly—two centuries before its time.

If Jones had any further ambitious plans for Greenwich, they were quickly shelved by a fire that destroyed an old Banqueting House in Whitehall and presented him with a gaudy commission: namely, to design a vast royal palace twice the size of Versailles. This and other grand designs were frustrated by the English Civil War.

However, when the monarchy was restored under Charles II, a devoted pupil of Jones, one John Webb, followed his master's Palladian plans and built a palace, known as King Charles's Block (lower right). This was no sooner up than London was consumed by the Great Fire of 1666.

Nothing more was done for the Greenwich project during the next thirty-odd years, until William and Mary turned to Sir Christopher Wren. His talents had been diverted, to say the least, by his commissions to re-design St. Paul's and replace fifty gutted churches, but now he was free to build the other three Greenwich blocks and incorporate the Queen's House in the final symmetrical plan you are looking down on.

Just a minute or two after high noon, at the top of the picture, you can see peeping out from a ring of woods the original Royal Observatory, built in 1675 to help seamen determine their positions at sea. In 1884, an international conference of astronomers in Washington, D.C. laid down that a line passing through the Greenwich Observatory should be the prime meridian of the earth. Since then, a time-ball has descended at precisely 1 p.m. every day to signify the mean time that defines the exact time in the earth's twenty-four time zones.

Next to the Royal Naval College is the terminal pier of the river launches and above it the last of the British clipper ships, the CUTTY SARK, which is now a merchant marine educational center and a maritime museum. Below the glass dome atop a pedestrian subway, and just in view in the right-hand corner, is the GYPSY MOTH, the tiny yacht in which Francis Chichester sailed alone round the world and came home to port and a knighthood.

The avenue of chestnut trees that runs in the direction of the Queen's House marks the center of GREENWICH PARK laid out as a royal park for Charles the Second by Louis the Fourteenth's landscape gardener.

And south again is the great common of BLACK-HEATH, in the 14th and 15th centuries the base of operations for rebels like Wat Tyler and Jack Cade and at all times a rallying point for highwaymen. The cluster of houses at the southeast is MONTPELIER ROW. It was designed about 1800 and rebuilt after bomb damage. Adjoining it are brick almshouses built by Wren.

To put an end to a thriving Anglo-American controversy, it can be said categorically that the oldest golf club in the world, the Blackheath Golf Club, was founded here in 1608 but later removed to Eltham, Kent, appropriately the birthplace of a struggling 15-handicapper named Leslie Townes (Bob) Hope.

Apartment houses (British 'blocks of flats') in Packing Case Modern frown on what is left of the squalid but famous stretch of the river, LIMEHOUSE REACH, immortalized by Dickens in the opening chapter of *Our Mutual Friend*.

The *Double Diamond* beer sign is affixed to *The Grapes*, which is generally supposed to be the original of the *Six Jolly Fellowship Porters*, the inn in the same novel. Alongside it is a row of houses which, remodeled with new windows and garden terraces, are meant to suggest an island of chic in a waste of refuse dumps, rotting wharves and a barge repair yard. One of them, next to *The Grapes*, was considered smart enough to provide a home for Dr. David Owen, the Labor government's most recent Foreign Secretary.

(OPPOSITE) Behind the severe little modern hotel (just above the left pylon of the bridge) a brave effort is being made to convert St. Katherine Dock into a world trade center overlooking a marina, complete with various antique craft, a naval museum, a Dickens tavern, and several restored dockmaster's houses.

Although the landward limit of the Port of London Authority is at Teddington Lock, far upstream beyond Richmond, the thirty-odd miles of what might be called "the commercial river" virtually end at TOWER BRIDGE. Here we look back east on the last stretch of it, where the Lower Pool swings north into Limehouse Reach.

On the north bank, immediately left of Tower Bridge, are ST. KATHERINE DOCKS and, adjoining, the LONDON DOCK, which was opened with great fanfare in 1808. Both of them are now closed, victims—like two-thirds of the dock berths in the Pool of London over the past dozen years—of the radical change from conventional cargo to containers. Both these docks were once the great storage houses of wool, marble, tobacco, tea, rubber, sugar, coffee, spices and (London Dock especially) of wine.

# THE CENTRAL CITY

Down its nine centuries, the TOWER OF LONDON has been a formidable complex of royal palace, arsenal, state prison and always a fortress, never captured to this day.

William the Conqueror built it to protect London from the eastern approach by sea, as Windsor by land from the west. The original is the central, or WHITE, TOWER, with a massive Norman chapel that is the oldest piece of church architecture in England. The Tower was enlarged and elaborated by succeeding monarchs and is, in fact, a fortress of 22 towers, thirteen of them in the wall that encloses the Inner Ward, and another eight pro-

tecting the Outer Ward. Although the moat was drained and overlaid with a lawn in Victoria's day, most of the battle and hunting weapons (from the crossbow to the elephant gun) are still on show, and so are the mediaeval devices of torture.

No other building, or group of buildings, in the kingdom embodies so much that is regal and gruesome in the history of England. The Crown Jewels (most of those collected before 1660 were enthusiastically melted down by Cromwell) still glitter here. Ancient walls are scarred with heart-breaking graffiti by royal prisoners awaiting execution. The roll-call of kings, queens, princes, prin-

cesses, statesmen, courtiers, scholars, soldiers and bishops who were imprisoned or executed here is interminable, from the beginning of the 14th century to the middle of the 20th. Rudolf Hess was imprisoned here in 1941.

William the Conqueror's intention was to impress the citizens of London with the conviction that he was here to stay and would defend them against all their enemies. A tour of the Tower's trophies, artifacts, and barbarous relics leaves one, even today, wth the Duke of Wellington's passing thought: "They may not frighten the enemy but, by God, sir, they frighten me."

(OPPOSITE) This was taken at the end of a golden summer's day. But by a trick of halation, due to filming against the light, we see the London River as it truly appeared too often in the dark and smoggy days before the city, from the late 1950s, banished the burning of soft coal and all other smoky fuels, immobilized a million chimney pots and by 1970 had transformed the legendary Fog City into one of the cleanest of modern metropolises.

TOWER BRIDGE, perhaps because of its proximity to the ancient Tower of London, is often thought to be one of London's more venerable symbols. It is, in fact, a piece of very late Victorian Gothic, put up in 1894, three years after London's first telephone link with Paris.

An army of workmen and £1½ million succeeded, however, in fulfilling its intention, which was to dominate the river more than any other single bridge.

(OPPOSITE) London has been less mindful of its earliest treasures than most capital cities. It is hard to believe that SOUTHWARK (on the south bank just past London Bridge) is the most ancient part of the city or that here, lassoed by sweeping railroad tracks and hemmed in by warehouses, honeycomb high rises, the borough market and mean buildings of the past two centuries is the jewel of SOUTHWARK CATHEDRAL, the earliest Gothic work in London and by common consent the finest after Westminster Abbey.

Originally, in the 7th century, a nunnery, it was rebuilt as a church in 1106 and remodeled again and again. Among its incomparable works are the choir and retrochoir (1207), the altar screen (1520) and majestic tombs in the aisles. Shakespeare and the Globe players knew it as their local church, and John Fletcher, Philip Massinger and Shakespeare's younger brother are buried here.

It has interesting American associations. There is a miniature monument to one William Emerson, who died in 1575 and is supposed to be an ancestor of Ralph Waldo Emerson. John Harvard, the founder of Harvard College, was born in Southwark and baptized in the cathedral in 1607.

(RIGHT) It should be plain that this picture was not shot from any aesthetic urge. We are again south of the river in the somber clutter of Southwark. We leave you, however, to look and marvel at the squat brown building with the gambrel roofs (center). This has been identified as the SITE OF THE GLOBE THEATER, which was built by Burbage in 1599 and in which fifteen of Shakespeare's plays were first performed.

(OPPOSITE) Going across the river to the north, only an obsessed financier, or the most unflagging tourist, would want to go poking for long through the stone and concrete jungle of "THE CITY."

Dead center, in the angle of Prince's Street (west) and Threadneedle Street (south) is the BANK OF ENGLAND. Its sharp angle points across the road to the MANSION HOUSE, the official residence of the Lord Mayor, built in the 1740s. Across from the Bank (southeast) is the ROYAL EXCHANGE, which conducts no exchange business whatsoever but is entirely devoted to selling insurance. But the seven-sided skyscraper that rises to the northeast is the NEW STOCK EXCHANGE.

For the antiquary, however, there are two treasures buried deep amid the sticks and stones. First (upper left) with the sloping roof and the sharp pinnacles, is GUILDHALL, the ceremonial headquarters of the City of London.

It is a happy combination of Gothic and classical, with a majestic 15th century hall, skillfully repaired after the Blitz; 18th century windows by George Dance; and a wealth of sculptured memorials to such as Nelson, Wellington, the Elder Pitt, and Churchill. Its library, of nearly 200,000 books and manuscripts, is the richest reference source on London life and lore.

The other precious needle in the haystack, visible as a spire and a light blue dome behind the Mansion House, is ST. STEPHEN, WALBROOK, a small masterpiece of Wren done almost as a miniature of St. Paul's while he was designing the Cathedral. The noble dome, having eight arches supported on Corinthian columns, was an actual cartoon or rehearsal for the masterwork.

Nobody, except some of the people who live there, has a good word to say for THE BARBICAN, an ambitious attempt of the early 1960s to build "a commercial zone and a residential and cultural area" on 60 acres, in the densest part of the city, that was devastated by bombing in the Second World War.

It has been variously described as a cross between a mediaeval fortress and the worst of Le Corbusier, "a giant stride of cellular giant slabs," and "a mass of concrete in derivative styles." The masses or monoliths are linked by elevated walkways open, unfortunately, to the wind and rain, and end in "shapeless unusable corners." These bleak agglomerations of concrete are punctuated by rectangles of water whose function is a mystery to the sometime visitor. However, there are young residents who say that the concrete jungle will be lightened and civilized by the proposed addition of a Shakespeare Theater, a symphony concert hall, a lending library and a students' hostel. In the meantime, a cultural note is attempted by the naming of the three main towers after eminent men who had some association with the neighborhood: (reading from left to right) Lauderdale, Shakespeare and Cromwell.

43

Hemmed in (left to right) by the Cromwell and Shakespeare skyscrapers of THE BARBICAN are two old relics of London life and a new museum which displays an incomparable collection of the city's history from prehistoric times to the present.

This is one of the few places where Londoners can be grateful for the Nazi Blitz, for in the sunken garden are now exposed the Roman level of the city wall and, above it, bolsterings in grey stone from the 14th century and red brick topping from the 15th. To the right of the garden and overshadowing it is the above-mentioned MUSEUM OF LONDON, which deserves to be an early and compulsory stop on the tourist's itinerary.

Left center, partly obscured by 'Cromwell' (left) and the severe structure of the City of London's Girls' School (right) is a quiet plaza and above it the ancient church of ST. GILES WITHOUT CRIPPLEGATE (one of the five gates—Aldgate, Bishopsgate, Cripplegate, Newgate, and Ludgate which the Romans built to contain and defend the original city within a circumference of two miles.)

The first church was built in 1390. Fires and the crowding of the dead in the Great Plague caused several additions, and alterations into the 18th century. Finally, the church was hit in the first Nazi air raid on London and further damaged in December, 1940. But the whole building has been lovingly restored. Lancelot Andrewes, who helped translate the Bible into the King James version, was the vicar here. Shakespeare saw his nephew baptized here, Cromwell was married here, and Milton is buried here. And here also one Thomas Stagg achieves immortality through his succinct epitaph: "That is all."

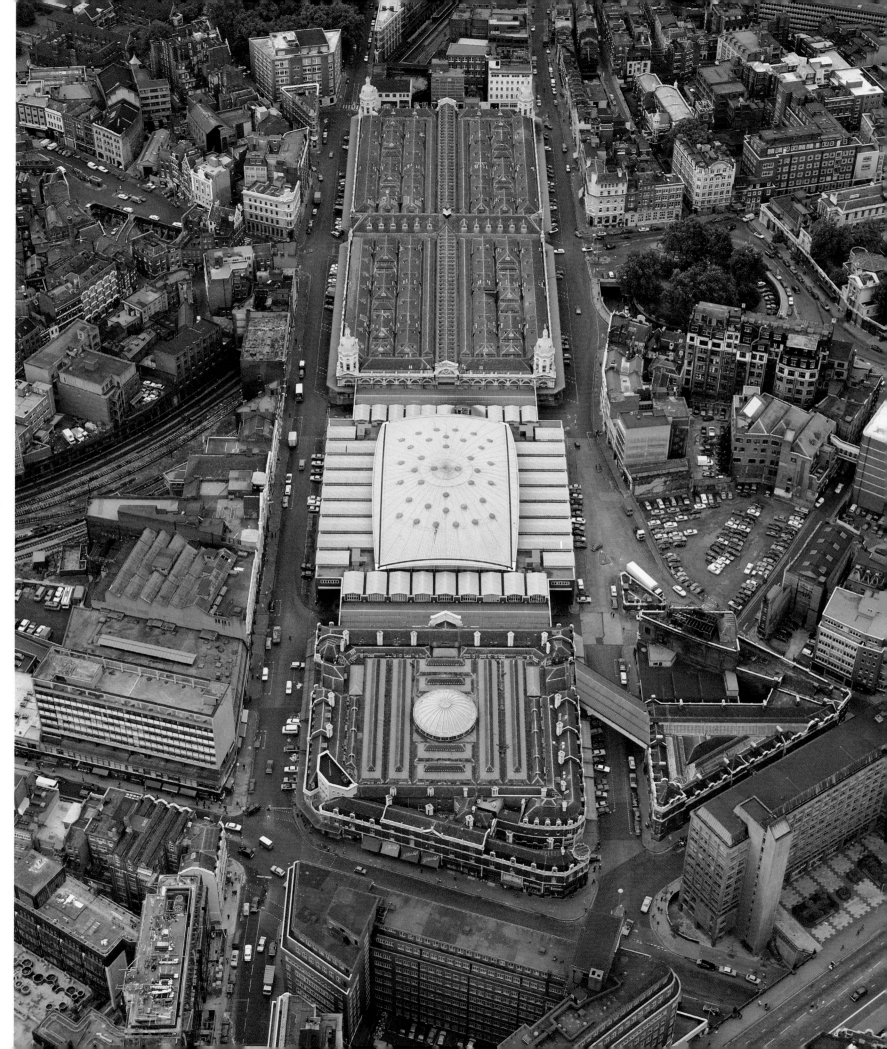

This is not a trade center, railroad station or convention hall but the main meat market of London: the CENTRAL MARKETS at SMITHFIELD (rebuilt in 1886) a corruption of "smooth field", a wide piece of grassland that once bordered the limits of the City Walls.

It has a long and gamey history, for not only was it for seven hundred years, (from the middle of the 12th century to the middle of the 19th), the main horse and cattle market of London but for a couple of hundred years—from the beginning of the 14th century—a principal place of execution for secular rebels and Protestant martyrs.

From north to south, the four huge buildings of the market are divided by Grand Avenue, East Poultry Avenue and West Poultry Avenue.

Off (upper right) to the east of the little circular park is the wall of ST. BARTHOLOMEW'S HOSPITAL, founded in 1123, but fortunately modernized many times since. Probably the first free hospital in England, it is now the most famous medical school in the British Isles. It contains an octagonal church, a splendid hall by James Gibbs, and some distinguished paintings by Hogarth. Medically, it is most renowned for William Harvey, a Kentish man who graduated M.D. from Padua, then from Cambridge, who was for 34 years chief physician, and who in 1616 announced his revolutionary, and widely resisted, theory of the circulation of the blood.

Swinging east through the Blackfriars Underpass, White Lion Hill curves up into the invisible Godliman Street, which leads directly to the south facade of ST. PAUL'S CATHEDRAL. It was one of the pleasures peculiar to flying in a helicopter on a clear night that one could see St. Paul's as the majestic and isolated jewel Wren intended it to be by day, and not as (OPPOSITE) a noble dome struggling for recognition above an undergrowth of buildings of every shape and period.

Here, west of Blackfriars Bridge are moored four ships. In the foreground, the *DISCOVERY*, Captain Scott's polar research ship; beyond, the *WELLINGTON,* the *CHRYSANTHEMUM* and the *PRESIDENT.* Three of them are naval and marine training ships. The *Wellington* has the distinction of being the only floating headquarters of a City Livery Company.

Two streets back from the river, between the *Discovery* and the *Wellington* can be seen a red-bricked mansion in the Tudor style which was built for the late Lord Astor and is now an overseas telegraph office. Beyond are the Middle and Inner Temples and their surrounding gardens.

(OPPOSITE) Above the four ships and the Embankment is a spacious and private maze of buildings, cloisters, alleys and gardens that enclose the very English sanctuary of the Law: THE INNS OF COURT. Two of them are out of sight, north of the Strand, but here are the Middle and Inner Temples and their gardens.

If the whole looks more like a university than a law school, that is no accident. Through the 15th and 16th centuries, lawyers, students and apprentices marked out this pleasant riverfront as their communal home, where they ate, studied, slept, worshiped, argued and socialized. To this day, there are flats for lawyers and some non-lawyers, and aspirants to the Bar must eat three dinners a term. High Court judges feast here, and the Inns are still the examining body of the law.

The MIDDLE TEMPLE around the smaller garden (left) and the INNER TEMPLE around the larger were both bombed during the Second War but have been scrupulously restored. A fine example is the Middle Temple Hall (left center with the flagpole) built in the 1560s. A great rarity, bombed but exquisitely restored, is the ROUND CHURCH (upper right center) built in 1185. It is one of only five other mediaeval round churches left in England. They were all built as models of the Holy Sepulchre in Jerusalem (whose desecration by the Muslims in the 11th century provoked the 400-year war of the Crusades).

(RIGHT) After almost a century of yearning, controversy, and withering comparisons with the cultural enlightenment of Europe, the British intelligentsia got, in 1976 what it had for so long been pleading for: a NATIONAL THEATRE (on the south bank, across from the four ships).

It includes three theaters: the Olivier, named after the acknowledged master of the profession; the Lyttleton, named after the late Lord Chandos, an old campaigner for the cause; and Cottesloe, for smaller experiments.

There was much complaint in the beginning about the starkness of the architectural design, but the handsomeness of the interiors eventually silenced its critics. Even so, it is much more of a harmonious unit seen from the air than it is seen from the ground.

Upstream from the National Theatre and across Waterloo Bridge is the ROYAL FESTIVAL HALL, designed by Sir Leslie Martin and Sir Robert Matthew. What might be looked on in Dallas, say, as a rather pedestrian block was considered, during the euphoria of the Festival of Britain (1951) it celebrated, a masterpiece of London modern. However, its concert hall is at once spectacular and simple, and its splendid acoustics have made it the home of the London Symphony and the London Philharmonic orchestras.

Adjoining it to the left and linked by terraces are two architecturally incongruous neighbors: on the riverfront, the stark QUEEN ELIZABETH HALL, another concert hall, and behind it the HAYWARD GALLERY, used for loan exhibitions.

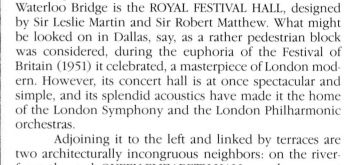

Unless your primary interest is in oil stocks or hotels, the appeal of this picture will not be in the massive whiteface of the Shell-Mex building and its huge clock, or in the Savoy Hotel across the street but in the curious obelisk, guarded by two prone bronze sphinxes, on the edge of the Embankment.

It is misleadingly called CLEOPATRA'S NEEDLE, though she had never heard of it. It was presented to Britain in 1819 by the Egyptian viceroy, one Mohammed Ali (no relation). It is one of two monoliths of pink granite built in 1500 B.C. in Heliopolis (the "sun city" of Egypt) by Thothmes the Third, whose heroic deeds are inscribed on the Needle's sides.

The story of its passage from the Nile delta to London is a masterpiece of bureaucratic incompetence. It was mislaid, burnt, broken, sunk at sea, salvaged, and only after sixty years at last planted by the Thames. Its twin is in New York City's Central Park.

50

The vast Palladian structure of SOMERSET HOUSE, facing the river and backing onto the Strand, stands on the site of a 16th century palace built for the Duke of Somerset, the "protector" of the child king, Edward the Sixth. It was subsequently the home of Elizabeth the First as a princess, and of the wives of James the First, and the two Charleses.

It was demolished in 1766 and within the next twenty years the present buildings went up, to the designs of Sir William Chambers, to house every sort of public record, as well as the Admiralty, the Royal Society and the Royal Academy. Until fairly recently, it was possible, for a pittance, to inspect the wills and testaments of Englishmen from the middle of the 14th Century on. But these, and many other records, began to burst their files and were transferred to the Public Record Office. It is still possible, though, to see what Lord Nelson and Dickens, among other celebrities, left to their heirs and assigns.

The south wing, facing the river, is given over to the forbidding records, by way of taxes and death duties, of the Board of Inland Revenue.

At the northeast corner, obscured by a Steamboat Modern building, is the spire and facade of ST. MARY-LE-STRAND, which is expertly considered to be the masterpiece of James Gibbs in the full flush of his enthusiasm for the Roman style. Inside and out, it is an exquisite little church and a strangely silent refuge from "the roaring traffic's boom."

What Gothic fantasist, either original or revived, could have thought up this daydream, or nightmare, as a railroad station? The answer is: none. It was designed by Sir George Gilbert Scott in the 1860s to be the new Foreign Office, but the design was rejected and it came to gaudy life on the Euston Road as ST. PANCRAS STATION.

Seen from the ground it towers confidently above two mockers: the compact white building (1973) of Camden Town Hall, and, in the right bottom corner, the modern roof and surmounting arch of King's Cross station.

(OPPOSITE) BATTERSEA POWER STATION, on the south bank and close to the reclaimed marshland that made Battersea Park, blew up a storm of protest while it was being built, in the early 1930s. But since it had been designed by Sir Giles Gilbert Scott, a famous ecclesiastical architect, the aesthetes retired in bafflement and the general public came to take to it as to a lovable monster. During the Second World War it was jealously guarded by the night-time firewatchers.

Since river pollution became a lively public concern, the biggest power stations are now well downstream, where the water is colder and thermal pollution is easier to control.

The Battersea station is shortly to be closed down. At this writing, its most useful function seems to be to pipe hot water under the river to heat the thirty-odd blocks of flats of CHURCHILL GARDENS, the first big municipal housing project to go up after the war. It was started in the bleak winter of 1946, a time of deprivation worse than that of the war itself, since the United States abruptly stopped all Lend-Lease aid immediately after the surrender of Japan. In the following years of rationing and other pinches of austerity, the Gardens took sixteen years to finish.

BATTERSEA PARK, west of the power station, is not quite the festive pleasure ground it was during the 1951 Festival of Britain. A bad accident on the Big Dipper, erected on what is now just an empty circle (right center) may have had something to do with scaring people off. It is a pleasant place nonetheless, a green haven in the industrial desert of the south bank. It has a tropical garden, playing fields, a boating lake and some sculpture by Henry Moore.

(OPPOSITE) BATTERSEA POWER STATION, on the south bank and close to the reclaimed marshland that made Battersea Park, blew up a storm of protest while it was being built, in the early 1930s. But since it had been designed by Sir Giles Gilbert Scott, a famous ecclesiastical architect, the aesthetes retired in bafflement and the general public came to take to it as to a lovable monster. During the Second World War it was jealously guarded by the night-time firewatchers.

Since river pollution became a lively public concern, the biggest power stations are now well downstream, where the water is colder and thermal pollution is easier to control.

The Battersea station is shortly to be closed down. At this writing, its most useful function seems to be to pipe hot water under the river to heat the thirty-odd blocks of flats of CHURCHILL GARDENS, the first big municipal housing project to go up after the war. It was started in the bleak winter of 1946, a time of deprivation worse than that of the war itself, since the United States abruptly stopped all Lend-Lease aid immediately after the surrender of Japan. In the following years of rationing and other pinches of austerity, the Gardens took sixteen years to finish.

BATTERSEA PARK, west of the power station, is not quite the festive pleasure ground it was during the 1951 Festival of Britain. A bad accident on the Big Dipper, erected on what is now just an empty circle (right center) may have had something to do with scaring people off. It is a pleasant place nonetheless, a green haven in the industrial desert of the south bank. It has a tropical garden, playing fields, a boating lake and some sculpture by Henry Moore.

This picture, taken in the long twilight of a fine early autumn day, was frankly enjoyed for itself, for the mellow light that softens the harsh agglomerations of styles and isolates one building (the skyscraper left center) as a structure that would not be unworthy of a home in Dallas, Houston or Atlanta.

We are looking down on Soho, and—to the left of the skyscraper—Bloomsbury, which—improbably—nursed the rarified talents of Virginia Woolf and Lytton Strachey. The late light almost obliterates the sense of place, so that even native Londoners were able to place Tottenham Court Road or St. Giles's Circus only because the famous skyscraper rises above them. It is CENTREPOINT, and might well be called The White Elephant which, since it went up in 1964, has (like the Empire State Building during the Depression) attracted few tenants.

53

This most un-English looking contraption, whose radar aerial seems to be touching a church on Albany Street, is the POST OFFICE TOWER, 580 feet high, with a 40 foot mast: the second tallest building in Britain.

It was designed for television and radio-telephony and was finished in 1965. Its appeal for the tourist lies in a revolving restaurant, on the 34th floor, from which you can look west and see Windsor Castle and look directly down on FITZROY SQUARE, which was started by the Adam brothers, which was the home of George Bernard Shaw in the 1890s, and which—in an age when medical specialties are described with pompous Latinisms—houses the simple amenity of "The London Foot Hospital."

(OPPOSITE) The point of this picture is not the bottom corner view of the roofs of the National Gallery and the National Portrait Gallery, nor the glimpse of Trafalgar Square, nor St. Martin in the Fields, nor yet the hotel fronting the railroad station in the center—but the tiny spire in the courtyard dead center, and any emotions that might be roused by the thought that here in 1291, Edward the First put down the last of the thirteen crosses that were set up along the way of a funeral procession for his Queen Eleanor that started in Nottinghamshire and wended its solemn way one hundred and thirty miles south to Westminster Abbey. The present monument houses a replica (1865) of the original cross.

CHARING CROSS is regarded, if not as Dr. Johnson's "full tide of human existence," as the central point of London from which all distances are measured.

It is something of a tribute to the British determination not only to survive but to survive in their old quarters that we see the HOUSES OF PARLIAMENT today looking much as they did in 1850, when Londoners—weary of the grace and austerity of a royal city that seemed to have been designed exclusively by the worldly John Nash—re-fashioned their government in an orgy of Gothic (or, as it was called Christian) architecture.

The Houses of Parliament sit on what was once the royal palace of Edward the Confessor, who died in 1066. During the next 800 years, the Lords and then the Commons suffered from plots, counter-plots, enforced changes of site, and several damaging fires, the worst of which happened in 1834, when the whole place was destroyed, except for a crypt and WESTMINSTER HALL (center, just to the right of NEW PALACE YARD and its catalpa trees). The Hall, a late 14th century legacy from Richard the Second, is a somber place topped by a magnificent hammer beam roof.

The 1834 disaster was thought of, by two architects at least, as a god-sent opportunity to redeem the city from the godless, if picturesque, inventions of Nash. One of them was Sir Charles Barry, who designed the exterior. The other was Augustus Pugin, son of a French immigrant and a Roman Catholic convert, who published, two years after the fire, a passionate pamphlet attacking the "meanness and vulgarity" of Nash and other classicists and making a plea for a general Gothic revival. He was given the job of decorating the interior of the new Houses and he went at it with brilliant industry for over a decade, furnishing everything from the altars, screens, stained glass and Gothic facades down to mediaeval inkstands.

A hundred years later, the worst blow fell: on the 10th of May, 1941, the House of Commons was almost totally destroyed by Nazi bombs. Whereupon, it was painstakingly rebuilt, by the gospel according to Barry and Pugin, though its interior has strikingly inferior woodwork that would have embarrassed Pugin. Still, there it is, probably the most successful example of the Victorian Gothic revival, harmoniously adapted to the prototype of Westminster Hall. The graceful CENTRAL SPIRE is a ventilating shaft, flanked on the left by the HOUSE OF COMMONS and on the right by the HOUSE OF LORDS. At the end, overshadowing the river gardens, is VICTORIA TOWER, the tallest (336 ft.) square tower that exists.

Directly in front of Westminster Hall is ST. MARGARET'S CHURCH, rebuilt in the early 1500s and since the 17th century the "parish church" of the House of Commons (Pepys, Milton and Churchill were married here).

To the right of St. Margaret's towers WESTMINSTER ABBEY, about which any caption running to less than several thousand words would be pitifully inadequate. Suffice it to say that it is an anthology of English church architecture from the 13th to the late 19th century; that most English sovereigns from Edward the Confessor to George the Second lie buried here, and every sovereign—except Edward the Fifth and Edward the Eighth—was crowned here; and that it is a national mausoleum commemorating with tombs, slabs, medallions, statues, statuettes and busts the eminent dead whose bones lie here or who have been thought worthy of a memorial plaque: a vast silent assembly of sovereigns, statesmen, authors, di-

vines, doctors, artists, actors, engineers, musicians, bridge-builders, empire builders and so on and on.

To the right of the Abbey are the deanery, chapter house, various cloisters and gardens and (at four o'clock) an open courtyard—Dean's Yard—enclosed by the buildings of WESTMINSTER SCHOOL, one of the leading public (i.e. private) schools founded by Queen Elizabeth the First.

(OVERLEAF) The view looking to the Northwest from the river shows, beyond PARLIAMENT SQUARE (the central green lawn), the Foreign and other government offices, standing between St. James's Park and WHITEHALL, which runs up to William Kent's clock tower overlooking the HORSE GUARDS PARADE, where the sovereign's official birthday is celebrated every June with the highly theatrical ceremony of Trooping The Color.

Beyond the parade ground, and across the corner of St. James's Park, are the dazzling white facades of Nash's CARLTON HOUSE TERRACE at one end of the park, and Lancaster House at the other end.

The most interesting detail of this view is the little L-shaped building enclosed by a moat (just opposite Victoria Tower). It is the JEWEL TOWER, the last relic of the old Palace of Westminster built in the late 1300s by Henry Yevele, once mason to the Black Prince and, most famously, the designer of Westminster Hall. It is now a museum.

As W. S. Gilbert immortalized the head of the London Fire Brigade in *Iolanthe* ("Oh, Captain Shaw!"), so the Houses of Parliament have kept green the memory of a First Commissioner of Works: Sir Benjamin Hall, who was responsible for hanging "BIG BEN", a 13½ ton bell on which the hours are struck in the famous Clock Tower.

Since then (1859), however, Big Ben in popular usage has come to mean the clock itself, if not the Tower. The clock, which is wound by hand, has four 23 ft. square dials, with figures two feet high. The Tower is 320 ft. high. When a light shines in the Tower by night, the citizen knows that the House of Commons is exercising, as Gilbert put it, "its legislative hand."

# THE CITY–SOUTH AND WEST

On the south bank, just east of Lambeth Bridge, is LAMBETH PALACE, which appears on the earliest mediaeval maps as the home of the archbishop of Canterbury. So it has been for seven centuries, and though it was damaged in a 1941 air-raid, much of the early building stands, and the rest has been faithfully restored. It was started in 1207, and the original crypt beneath the chapel is intact. The red brick gatehouse, at the corner nearest to the river, was built in 1490. The Guard Chamber has portraits of the archbishops of the past five hundred years, notably ones by Holbein, Van Dyck, Hogarth, Reynolds, Romney and Sargent. The library, which is open to the public, has innumerable manuscripts and the odd prayer book belonging to such worthies as Queen Elizabeth the First, Francis Bacon, and Gladstone. The whole place is haunted by the ghosts of clerics, scholars and martyrs from Wyclif to Erasmus and Cranmer and Archbishop Laud.

The grounds beyond, called the Archbishop's Park, are open to the public. At the bottom, below the gatehouse, is the point where the archbishops embarked for the north bank. It is now a pier for the river police.

THE TATE GALLERY, a discreet, if lumpish, classical building at Millbank, between Lambeth and Vauxhall bridges, belies the date of its construction: 1897, when Victorian curlicues were all the vogue. It was commissioned by Sir Henry Tate, the sugar tycoon, who gave his own collection of sixty-five paintings to form the nucleus of a public collection. It has grown into one of the great galleries of Britain, or, for that matter, of Europe. Besides assembling the most comprehensive collection of British painting of the past 500 years, it has in the past 30 years added important collections of European and American painting, every "ism" of the 20th Century, and welcomes——sometimes with painful gravity—the wildest trivia of Pop and Op and whatever is to come after.

It also possesses—at this writing—the novelty, for an art gallery anywhere, of a fine restaurant. South of the Gallery (left) is the un-barracksy Millbank Barracks. North (right) is, first, the QUEEN ALEXANDRA MILITARY HOSPITAL and towering above it one of the half-dozen tallest buildings in London, the so-called VICKERS BUILDING (1963), which has both commercial and government (Department of Energy) office space.

Bang in the middle of Kennington (south of Vauxhall Bridge) a working-class district heavily bombed and more pleasantly rebuilt with blocks of flats, is THE OVAL, the home ground of the Surrey Country Cricket Club, which was formed almost a century and a half ago. The entrance gates are dedicated to the memory of the greatest batsman of his day (the 1910s and '20s), Jack (later Sir Jack) Hobbs.

Linking the Embankment and the eastern end of Battersea Park is CHELSEA BRIDGE, built as late as 1937. East of it, on the north bank, the Grosvenor Canal passes under the Embankment at a point near the tall chimney (left). The tracks of GROSVENOR BRIDGE carry trains into Victoria. Beyond (upper left) are the Churchill Gardens.

This is CHELSEA HOSPITAL, the home of the Chelsea Pensioners, the immortal or almost immortal (there are usually one or two centenarians among them) old and disabled soldiers, who may be seen, hale or tottering, wearing scarlet coats in summer and dark blue ones in winter.

It is one of the finer works of Sir Christopher Wren, and its foundation stone was laid by Charles the Second.

The Doric portico of the central building divides the Hall and the Chapel. The two wings are the dormitories. The curious skeleton colonnade close to the river was the first sign of the great tent that would soon enclose the famous May flower show.

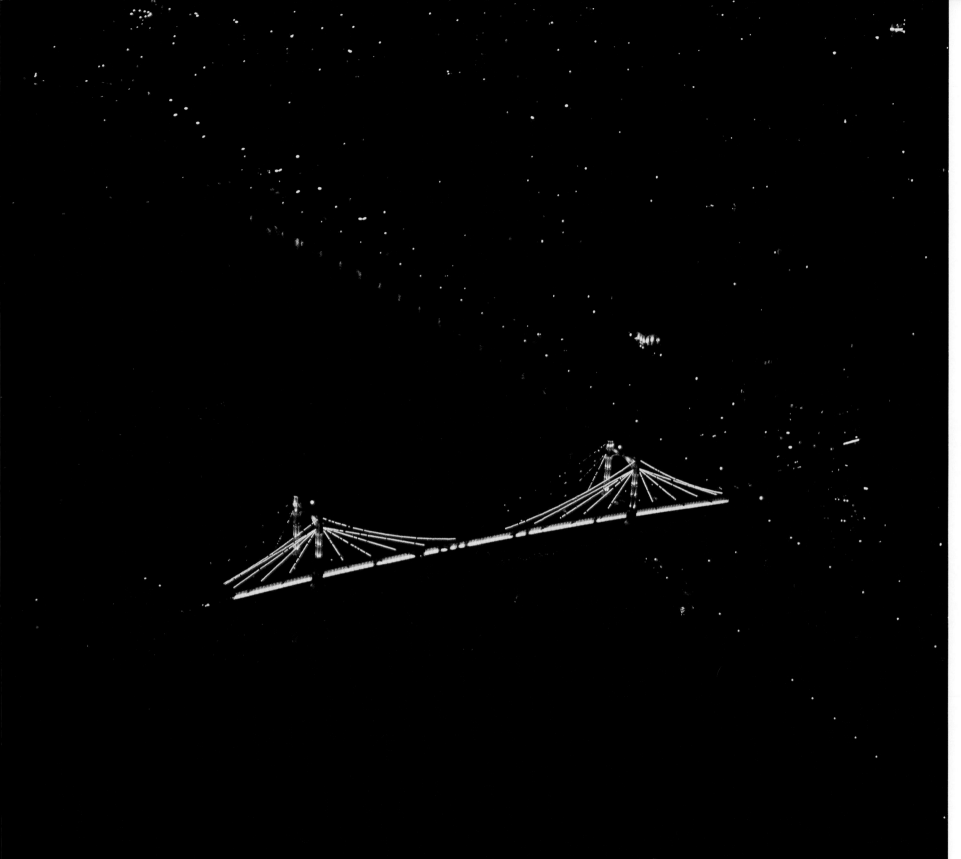

Yet another memorial to the Prince Consort, but a light-hearted one: ALBERT BRIDGE leading from the east end of Cheyne Walk to the entrance to Battersea Park.

The bridge's playful lattice work is well-suited to continuous chains of lights and adds a festival touch to a night crossing.

R. W. Ordish designed it, in 1873, as the river's first cantilever and suspension bridge. This daring innovation produced a rhythmic bounce which required troops to break step when crossing it.

(OPPOSITE) The community of people who live on houseboats and barges in Chelsea opposite CHEYNE WALK is thought by tourists to be one of the more picturesque features of London life. But not always by the Port of London Authority, which owns the river bed to the high-water mark and licenses moorings through the Chelsea Yacht and Boat Company.

As more and more applications come in from couples seeking to bypass the inflated real estate market, the PLA sees increasing problems of sewage and pollution, while the prosperous residents of Cheyne Walk see the floating houses as threats to the status value of a famous street.

Cheyne Walk runs from the corner of the brown apartment towers (upper left) down along the embankment well beyond Battersea Bridge (lower right). Behind it are council houses and blocks of flats built on a substantial part of old Chelsea that was badly bombed.

In the center of the main block facing the barges is LINDSEY HOUSE, a conspicuous white mansion, the only 17th Century Chelsea house still standing. It is flanked by what were once the homes of such as Brunel, the pioneer of bridge engineering, J. M. W. Turner, George Meredith, James McNeil Whistler, and Hilaire Belloc.

Due south of Chelsea, thirty-odd miles down the Brighton Road, is GATWICK, London's second airport, which handles mostly European traffic but now also some trans-Atlantic flights. No "second" airport was ever designed too big for its eventual load. As charter flights and package tours to the Continent have multiplied beyond everybody's expectations, the need for a third airport is desperate, and at this writing the argument over where it is to be sited rages on between planners and suburban householders.

Due north from Chelsea, in three city blocks between the southern fringe of Kensington Gardens and the Cromwell Road, is the museum trotter's heaven: the densest concentration in any city on earth of the applied arts, the sciences and technology: lovingly assembled collections of reptiles, musical instruments, fossils, armor, furniture, steam engines, whales, model cooling planets, the art of China, Islam and the Italian Renaissance, computers, jewels, miniature paintings and a quarter of a million butterflies.

The whole complex went up, in an explosion of Victorian curiosity and industriousness, in about thirty years in the second half of the 19th century.

Lower left is the long Romanesque facade of the NATURAL HISTORY MUSEUM, until fairly recently a soot-grimed monster but now cleaned to reveal with unsuspected grace the fineness of its terracotta detail.

Next to it, and across from the corner domes of the VICTORIA AND ALBERT MUSEUM (131 rooms of everything) is the GEOLOGICAL MUSEUM, the rarity of a

handsome piece of modern (1933) English architecture. Immediately behind it and linked by a roofed bridge is the SCIENCE MUSEUM.

The tall campanile, built to commemorate Queen Victoria's jubilee, is flanked on the left by the IMPERIAL COLLEGE OF SCIENCE AND TECHNOLOGY and on the right by the long, low buildings of the ROYAL COLLEGE OF MUSIC. Beyond it again is the ROYAL SCHOOL OF MINES pointing toward the glass dome of the ROYAL ALBERT HALL.

Captain Francis Fowke is the architect who is to be credited with this most successful and improbable of Victorian buildings. Resisting the contemporary mania for revived Gothic, he took his inspiration from the Roman works in Provence and finished in 1871 this huge amphitheater topped by a glass dome. It was originally called The Hall of Arts and Sciences but after the death of the Queen's consort was renamed THE ROYAL ALBERT HALL.

And fittingly so, since it crowns the great complex of Kensington science and industry museums which, in large part, owed their creation to the Prince's unflagging enthusiasm for technology.

It seats 8,000 people in comfort and is used for concerts, rallies, conferences and every sort of sporting event. North of it, inside Kensington Gardens, is the Albert Memorial (OVERLEAF).

By screaming contrast with the Albert Hall, the ALBERT MEMORIAL, conceded by its architect, Sir George Gilbert Scott to be "my masterpiece," is a Gothic trance. It took twelve years to build as a shrine to "a life devoted to the public good," and more than any other public tribute to the dead Consort it did something to assuage the ecstasy of Queen Victoria's grief.

Under the canopy, inlaid with agate, onyx, jasper, crystal and other precious stones, a 15 ft. bronze figure of the Prince ponders the catalogue of the Great Exhibition of 1851 he inspired. His pedestal is surrounded by 178 marble reliefs of artists and writers of many countries and all times. The four angles are decorated with allegorical groups representing Agriculture, Manufacture, Commerce and Engineering. At the four corners of the steps are other groups representing Europe, Asia, Africa and America: the whole intended to symbolize a world in mourning for the Great Impresario of useful knowledge.

After the First World War, a generation reacting against the gaudy excrescences of Victorian taste derided the Memorial as London's prime architectural horror. But now there is a generation ready to react against the austerities of modern building and look on the work with curiosity if not with awe. However that may be, such a thoroughgoing Victorian as Mark Twain wrote: "In all this grave and beautiful land, I have encountered only one genuinely humorous idea: the Albert Memorial."

KENSINGTON PALACE, on the western edge of Kensington Gardens, is the rather severe creation of Sir Christopher Wren, who did over the old house as the royal residence of William the Third. He was the first monarch to dislike and abandon the palace at Whitehall (none too soon, it burnt to the ground nine years later) preferring—as a rémedy for his wheezing bronchia—the clean air of a new house way off in the country. He moved in there in 1689, and for the next seventy years it was the home of the sovereign. But many other "royals" have lived and died here, and it is at present the home of Princess Margaret.

Princess Victoria was born here in 1819 and eight-een years later received here the news that she was the Queen. The State Apartments are open to the public and include Victoria's suite of rooms as well as many portraits from the royal collection.

Beyond the Palace grounds (center) is a line of mansions planned as a unit in 1843 but built (by Decimus Burton and Sidney Smirke) in a great range of styles. The Soviet and Czechoslovak embassies are housed here now. No. 8 was used, during the Second World War, to inter-rogate German prisoners of war. At the southern end, built at right angles to the main row and adjoining the Palace, is the first neo-Georgian house in London. It was designed by Thackeray himself, and he died there.

(OVERLEAF) At the latitude of Labrador, and 800 miles north of New York City, London enjoys a long sum-mer twilight and a sun that sets after ten p.m.

Here, as the sun goes over, Kensington is recog-nizable as the facade of the NATURAL HISTORY MUSEUM and the lanterned dome of the VICTORIA AND ALBERT. Beyond them lies the dark of Kensington Gardens and the lights of Paddington and Bayswater.

75

Adjoining Kensington on the east, and the gardens of Buckingham Palace on the west, is the lordly district of BELGRAVIA.

The high-toned prestige of Belgrave Square in relation to almost any other part of London was immortalized by W. S. Gilbert in a satirical quatrain that inverts the usual folk wisdom about the honesty of the poor:

*"Hearts just as brave and fair*
*May beat in Belgrave Square*
*As in the lowly air*
*Of Seven Dials."*

When he wrote that, Belgrave Square housed three dukes and a glitter of peers and baronets.

So late as 1825 it was a marsh. But when in that year George the Fourth asked John Nash to remodel Buckingham House, at the west end of St. James's Park, with the thought of making it the royal residence, the race to drain and fill in the swamp to the west became a genteel land rush: a rush, that is, to buy up housing sites from the landowner, Lord Grosvenor. Luckily, the time, the developer (Thomas Cubitt) and the architect (George Basevi) were perfectly matched. Cubitt produced a grand design that carried the Georgian style into a spacious grid plan of squares and crescents with classical white stucco facades, and behind them a charming—almost Spanish—maze of cottages and mews flats.

By the time it was finished, Queen Victoria had become the first royal occupant of Buckingham Palace, and soon a reaction set in against the graceful austerity of Georgian and Regency building. The Victorians were appalled at what one of them called "the wearisome ugliness" of Belgravia. But fortunately for some of us, they chose to practice their own wearisome floridities elsewhere.

Belgravia was remarkably unscarred by the Nazi bombs because, it was rumored in Berlin and Vichy, Air Marshal Goering had his eye on it as the proper setting for the London capital of the Third Reich.

Cubitt's Belgravia was built to last. Today it is unquestionably the most elegantly harmonious residential part of London, its mews flats cost the earth, many of its great houses are (invisibly) divided into apartments, and in the square no less than thirteen of the rest of them are foreign embassies.

The north end of the square is crowned by WILTON CRESCENT, while GROSVENOR CRESCENT curves off to the northeast. The two main blocks are divided in the middle by, respectively, Belgrave Mews North and Belgrave Mews South.

Belgrave Square (upper left) is here seen to be only a small part of Thomas Cubitt's grand design of Belgravia. The long rectangle of greenery that bisects EATON SQUARE (sic) is the King's Road. At its far northeast corner is ST. PETER'S, at one time the almost compulsory venue for the mating of debutantes and noble sprigs (or, later, the heirs of beer barons and other tycoons).

Eaton Square and its surrounding terraces and mews were laid out by Cubitt in the 1840s, between ten and fifteen years after he had finished Belgrave Square. He lived in the first cross street west of Eaton Square while he was supervising the whole project. At No. 88, Chopin gave his first London recital.

The tranquility of Eaton Place (facing the colonnade at the extreme left-hand corner of the Square) was disturbed in 1922, at the height of the Irish "troubles", when Sir Henry Wilson was shot dead on his own doorstep (No. 36) by Sinn Feiners. But during the American television run of *"Upstairs, Downstairs,"* tourists hot-footed it from Oxford and Stratford-upon-Avon to pay their respects to (the non-existent) 165, the fictional home of the Richard Bellamys.

The rear of Buckingham Palace and its gardens can be seen in the top right-hand corner.

The southern reach of Belgravia ends with the clatter and the clutter of railroad sheds of Victoria Station. But south again, the indefatigable Thomas Cubitt extended his stucco domain into Pimlico, lightening the facades of the north and south sides with two squares (ECCLESTON SQUARE at the top, WARWICK SQUARE at the bottom) and breaking the mass of the central block with the interesting novelty of a diagonal street, known as Warwick Way, which made possible two separate nests of variously shaped mews, first meant for stables and now for high-priced flats.

# THE CITY-NORTH AND WEST

PICCADILLY CIRCUS, a junction of streets that lead to all points of the compass, is always recommended to tourists as the hub of the West End and the place to start a tour of its theaters and night life. It is the Times Square of London and for many generations has been the obvious center for raucous celebrations of New Year's Eve, the Oxford and Cambridge boat race, Cup Final victories, and the ends of wars.

In the past fifty years, there have been countless plans to re-design the Circus as an elegant plaza worthy of the place that was once known as the Hub of Empire. They have all come to nothing, and today—what with its pushers in the Underground station, its garish ads, its sleazy amusement arcades and loitering junkies—it had better be called the Hub of Porn. The night-time bird's-eye view offers a mere splotch of light amid a surrounding gloom that blessedly masks the raffishness of the scene on the ground.

(OPPOSITE) The long curve of REGENT STREET (known as the Quadrant) begins at Piccadilly Circus, straightens out before Oxford Street to end at John Nash's ALL SOUL'S CHURCH. The street was built by Nash in the decade after 1813 as a *camino real*, a royal road between the Prince Régent's home at Carlton House in St. James's Park and the land he had bought which was to become Regent's Park.

Its graceful stucco houses and linking colonnades provided an incomparable example of the English genius—in the 18th and early 19th centuries—for accommodating elegant architecture to the human scale. The destruction of Nash's Regent Street in the mid-1920s was properly regarded as an artistic crime, and it is one that flourishes wherever a crescent or a Georgian row stands in the way of "progress": i.e. some developer's plan for an office block, a motorway, a new hotel.

Regent Street is now a vast bazaar. The garden oasis is GOLDEN SQUARE, with office buildings devoted mainly to the woolen trade. The tiny figure implanted in the center flower bed is George the Second, Handel's patron, in antique dress.

UPPER REGENT STREET winds into Langham Place and, across from Nash's ALL SOULS, (CENTER) the grey stone headquarters of the BRITISH BROADCASTING CORPORATION since 1931. This original, which at the time was considered both severe and huge, indecently dwarfing the Adam houses along Portland Place (upper left) was much too small to house the BBC's enormous post-war staff. It became necessary to take over the Langham Hotel (left center) and to erect beyond the main building a modern extension (seen above the needle point of All Soul's spire).

On the southeast edge of REGENT'S PARK a typical example of the melding of old and new done—as usual—not by design but by disaster. After heavy wartime bombing, a corner block of late Regency houses still stands, and so does HOLY TRINITY church, built in 1826, which is now the headquarters of the Society for the Promotion of Christian Knowledge. They are hemmed in by post-war apartment houses and (upper right) the headquarters of the ROYAL COLLEGE OF PHYSICIANS, a new building as handsome inside as out.

To the northwest, immediately over the trees, is the Park's spacious BROAD WALK, which goes to glory in May with its spaced flower gardens and its blossoming chestnuts.

(OPPOSITE) Go north from the BBC along Portland Place and you come on John Nash's PARK CRESCENT, a semi-circle of Ionic colonnades that he started in 1812 as a grand entrance to Regent's Park, which is flanked on its south side by great classical terraces, most of them also by Nash.

Marylebone Road divides the Crescent Gardens from PARK SQUARE GARDENS, which fringe the so-called Outer Circle and the southern entrance to Regent's Park itself.

(OPPOSITE) REGENT'S PARK was originally yet another of Henry the Eighth's hunting preserves, and until the end of the 18th century was leased to rich men for their "country" villas. Surprisingly few were built and in 1811 the Prince Regent took it over. To the great good fortune of later generations, he commissioned John Nash to lay it out as a royal pleasure garden, which was thrown open to the public in 1838.

Across the top of the picture we see the superb monumental terraces with which Nash flanked the southern end of the Park. Upper right is BEDFORD COLLEGE, the earliest (1849) of London's colleges for women, and beyond it we get a glimpse of a 22-acre artificial lake. The white building at the bottom is ST. JOHN'S LODGE, also a part of Bedford College.

Most of the park's great space (472 acres) is given over to cricket and other sports, but there is a profusion of wooded walks and unexpected nooks of willows and water and, always, flowers. The chief glory of the Park is this circular formal garden known as QUEEN MARY'S GARDENS, comprising a rosary, a lily pond, a Japanese rock garden (right center) ringed with conifers, and an open-air theater (lower right).

In early summer the air is dense with the scent of roses and the flight of birds both humble and exotic. Few capitals can boast in the inner city such a bosky and decorative haven from the roar of the metropolis.

It is not difficult to imagine the uproar in New York if the daughter of a British tycoon decided to annex several acres of Central Park for her private use and build a mansion on them.

There are Britons who have wondered at the seemingly similar audacity of Barbara Hutton, the Woolworth heiress, in using a parcel of Crown property for a "country villa." However, she was well within legal disposition of her acres, many more of which within the fringes of the Park had been long ago sold to private persons. Hers

had belonged to St. Dunstan's (a charitable foundation for the blind), which sold them to speculators who, in the early 1930s, built this Georgian-style WINFIELD HOUSE and looked around for a buyer. They found her in Miss Hutton, who lived here from 1936 until the outbreak of the Second World War.

Ten years later she presented the house and grounds to the United States government, which has used it ever since as the official residence of the American ambassador to the Court of St. James's.

(OPPOSITE) The Zoo (properly the ZOOLOGICAL GARDENS) covers 36 acres at the north end of Regent's Park and an extraordinary range of the animal kingdom.

It was founded by Sir Humphrey Davy (the inventor of the safety lamp) in 1826. It introduced the simulation of a natural habitat in 1913. In the early 1930s it took the first attractive leap into modern architecture with the Penguin Pool of Lubetkin (center, below the lawn), which later inspired the adjoining graceful ramps and gardens of the New Lion Terraces. During the last two decades, there has been a continuous spurt of attractive building (new ape pavilions, a modern aviary house, an institute of comparative physiology, an animal hospital) and much ingenious and pleasing work done on re-developing the gardens according to a master plan drawn up twenty years ago by Sir Hugh Casson.

Most conspicuous from the air (center) is the chic modern fortress of the Elephant and Rhinoceros Pavilion. But somewhere in this London folly, you will find houses set aside for a great variety of the stalking, leaping, flying, crawling denizens of our earth, not to mention a library of over 100,000 volumes in which to discover their habits.

Between the Outer Circle and Regent's Canal is a horizontal stretch of smaller buildings beginning (upper left) with horses and cattle and ending (upper right) with the Insect House (due southeast of the seven poplars).

The only landmark that can be seen from the embassy grounds—and an ever-present reminder of the new power of Islam—is the minaret of the new CENTRAL MOSQUE (built between 1954 and 1977) whose courtyard in summer is packed with Arabs at prayer.

If Regent's park is the grandest and most varied of London parks, ST. JAMES'S PARK (OPPOSITE) is certainly the most delightful, maybe because, of the three monarchs who owned it, two of them loved birds and flowers and spared no pain or ingenuity in making it a graceful place in which to stroll and meditate. (Charles the First, alas, strolled across it for the last time on the way to his execution).

Henry the Eighth drained this marshy land between the two palaces at St. James's (upper right) and Whitehall (running behind the Horse Guards' Parade whose roof juts into the lower left-hand corner) to make a deer forest for himself. It was trimmed and laid out with formal walks by Charles the First and remained the resort of the Court throughout his reign. It was Charles the Second, however, who made it what it is today. He employed the French landscape gardener, Le Nôtre, to restore it to an artful informality and plant its flower beds. Charles introduced, also, exotic ducks, geese, and pelicans, whose descendants strut around today. It was Charles who, very soon after the Restoration, threw this royal garden open to the public, a gesture that incited a French visitor to a derisive comment: "It is a strange sight...to see the flower of the nobility and the first ladies of the Court mingling in confusion with the vilest populace. Such is the taste of the English: it is part of what they call their liberty."

So it is today, with a Foreign Secretary taking his constitutional past German pelican-watchers, Japanese flower-photographers, and scattered Cockneys eating their lunchtime sandwiches on the grass.

George the Fourth got the tireless John Nash to add a few undulations and link an old Dutch canal and several little lakes into the single meandering lake we see today. From the air one appreciates better than from the ground the noble surroundings of these 93 acres: the Palace to the west, St. James's and the Mall to the north, Birdcage Walk to the South, and the Horse Guards Parade to the east. Unfortunately, the bird's-eye view in summer, while emphasizing the alternation of lawns and woods, does nothing to reveal the graceful willows, the splendor of the flower beds or the antics of the wildfowl.

A fish-eye view of WHITEHALL, ST. JAMES'S PARK, THE PALACE, the royal garden, and GREEN PARK grossly exaggerates the scale of the most elegant and royal part of London. But it also dramatizes the fact that when the royal palace was in Whitehall (left center), and before St. James's Park was given to the people, the monarchs created and possessed a green central city, complete with splendid palaces and vast gardens, beyond which the rest of the citizenry were dispersed at random round the rural periphery, or crammed into busy alleys south of the river.

(OPPOSITE) What the public sees of BUCKINGHAM PALACE is the rear end, the rather dour eastern facade, completely rebuilt in 1913. The front of the palace, the WESTERN FACADE, is a charming design of John Nash, the main building flanked by two little classical pavilions, the whole giving onto a spacious lawn and a sloping private garden of 40 acres, almost half as large as St. James's Park.

The original house, built for the Duke of Buckingham in 1703, was bought by George the Third sixty years later. It was passed on to George the Fourth who commissioned its radical remodeling by Nash and changed its name to Buckingham Palace. But it did not become the regular London residence of the Monarch until Queen Victoria moved in on her accession in 1837. Her first son, Edward the Seventh, was born and died here. Charles, the present Prince of Wales, was born here and so were his two younger brothers.

The only part of the Palace open to the public is the Queen's Gallery, (in the southwest wing) which puts on show changing selections of paintings and furniture from the royal collection.

Nowhere in England do more cameras click, on more mornings, in all weathers, than they do at 11:30 a.m. outside Buckingham Palace for the CHANGING OF THE GUARD. The old Palace guard has by then trooped the Queen's color from St. James's Palace and marched, with an accompanying band, to the Palace. There it joins another contingent of the old guard and on the stroke of 11:30 is replaced, in an elaborate and ancient ceremony, by a new guard, which has marched in with its own band from Chelsea Barracks.

(OPPOSITE) GREEN PARK lies, across Constitution Hill, just to the north of the Palace Gardens and is separated from St. James's Park (upper right) by the Mall's long avenue of plane trees. Green Park was added onto St. James's by Charles the Second and is, by London standards, a comparatively modest, informal stretch of undulating grass, trees and wildflowers. It is bounded on the north by Piccadilly and on the east by a narrow lane, QUEEN'S WALK, above which rises some of the most graceful domestic architecture in London. The walk begins at the northeast corner of the Park with the Ritz Hotel (the grey mansard roof), whose name—the Blue Guide sedately reminds us—"inspired an American epithet for luxurious living."

The Walk continues past one or two charming Georgian houses with gardens, and then—after the rather jarring interruption of three modern blocks of flats—a succession of splendid mansions, beginning with John Vardi's (1765) Spencer House, its beautiful Palladian facade crowned with white statues, and going on past Bridgewater House, a small Italian Renaissance palace, then a delightful bow-fronted Selwyn House built not during the Regency but, surprisingly, in 1895. The Walk ends at the corner of the Mall with the imposing sandstone pile of Lancaster house, which was designed for that skinflint Duke of York who achieved, but did not deserve, the distinction of the famous column. Lancaster house is now reserved for government receptions but is open to the public on summer weekends.

95

A reverse view of ST. JAMES'S from the northeast end of THE MALL looking toward Queen Victoria's memorial statue and Buckingham Palace.

From Lancaster House, at the corner of Queen's Walk, we see next the white-stuccoed Clarence House, built by Nash for William the Fourth and now the home of the Queen Mother. Then, St. James's Palace and its courtyards, and after the cross-street of Marlborough Road, the spacious lawns fronting Marlborough House, which was built by Wren for the most grandiloquent of the Churchills, the first Duke of Marlborough, and has—by order of his iron duchess—huge frescoes of his victories. At various later times, it has been lived in by Queen Adelaide, George the Fifth, Queen Alexandra and, most famously, by Edward the Seventh when he was Prince of Wales. It was then the hub of Edward's "Marlborough Set", whose tolerant and racy ways were much deplored by Queen Victoria.

The harmony of Wren's original has been jarred by later additions. To the right of the House and its grounds, we see PALL MALL, the street of clubs, running to the corner of St. James's street, which begins opposite the gateway of St. James's Palace. Behind its towers, we can just see an open court, called FRIARY COURT. From its balcony, each new sovereign is first proclaimed.

By night, the clutter of stone that surrounds TRA-
FALGAR SQUARE (SEE OVERLEAF) vanishes and leaves flood-
lights to define only the Nash building, Admiralty Arch,
the National Gallery, South Africa House, St. Martin in the
Fields, and the Strand looping off to the east. But Nelson
himself, in his languid one-armed stance, is almost more
conspicuous than he is by day.

The east end of the Mall is enclosed by the last of the Nash terraces (lower left), the massive New Admiralty, (lower right) finished in 1895 (now a civil service headquarters) and—in the center—ADMIRALTY ARCH, which was designed as a memorial to Queen Victoria.

At the extreme lower left, we can just see, at the top of steps rising from the Mall, THE DUKE OF YORK'S COLUMN, a Doric pile forty feet or more less than Nelson's Monument, but high enough—some wag of the day (1833) said—to keep him safe from his creditors. He was the second son of George the Third and a notorious skinflint whose memorial was appropriately financed by "stopping one day's pay from every soldier in the army."

(OPPOSITE) The archway leads into TRAFALGAR SQUARE, which was laid out by Nash and begun 25 years after Nelson was mortally wounded by a musket shot as he walked the quarter deck of his ship the Victory, during the Battle of Trafalgar (21st of Oct. 1805). In spite of lively protests in Parliament against bestowing any national honors on an admiral who had seduced the wife of Sir William Hamilton, had two illegitimate children by her, and begged the government in his will to regard her as "a legacy to my king and country" for whom "ample provision" ought to be made (the government left her nothing), he was nevertheless buried in St. Paul's in the coffin of a sarcophagus originally made at Cardinal Wolsey's expense for the burial of Henry the Eighth.

Ever since, Nelson has been regarded as the first of Britain's naval heroes. It took Nash twenty years to complete the Square. Two years later (1841), the NELSON MONUMENT went up, a 167½ foot Corinthian column surmounted by a 17½ foot statue of Nelson and guarded at its base by four bronze lions, each 20 feet long. Today the central square is a home for wheeling pigeons, protest rallies, and listless hippies.

The north end of the Square is flanked by the NATIONAL GALLERY, which started in 1824 with 38 pictures bought from a private collector and today houses, in 46 rooms, one of the world's great gatherings of paintings of many schools, from the middle of the 13th century through the French Impressionists.

At the east end is the seven-story South Africa House, designed in 1933 by Sir Herbert Barker. And just across Duncannon Street, to the north, is the church of ST. MARTIN IN THE FIELDS, finished in 1724 when it towered over pasture and meadowland. It is considered the major masterpiece of James Gibbs, as St. Mary-le-Strand is the minor. Francis Bacon, John Hampden and Charles the Second were christened here. A mark of its later fame was its choice by the BBC as the first place from which to broadcast an "outside" religious service.

To top a classical portico with a steeple was considered in its day a daring novelty. One critic has remarked that "it has been often copied, but less successfully." He might have added: "Except throughout New England, where charming and graceful variations in wood, on this model, abound."

(OPPOSITE) This enormous vista embraces practically the whole of MAYFAIR, long regarded as the most socially chic district of London, if not—as Sydney Smith contended over a century ago—a region that "enclosed more intelligence and ability, to say nothing of wealth and beauty, than the world had ever collected into such a space before." (19th century Englishmen were no more reticent than 20th century Americans in proclaiming that whatever was home-grown was the best and brightest in the world).

The monolith that just intrudes (lower left) on this packed domestic scene is the London Hilton hotel, much resented at the time it went up. The view is bounded on the west by Park Lane, on the north by the Bayswater Road and Oxford Street, on the south by Shepherd Market, and on the east by Berkeley Square, whose full summer foliage happily obscures the featureless office blocks and automobile showrooms that have despoiled what was once an architectural gem and a sanctuary for that famous nightingale.

The place got its name from a fair held since 1688 during the first week in May. Into its marshy land to the north came men hired by the butchers to hunt ducks with dogs. To the south (below the ring of trees that festoon Crewe House on Curzon Street) is the village in a city known as SHEPHERD MARKET. And here flocked such a collection of con men, trollops, footpads, and cutthroats that within twenty years of the first fair, a Westminster grand jury urged "those in Power and Authority" to do something "to rectify...the great corruption and debauchery, (the) riots, tumults, breaches of the peace, open and notorious lewdness and murder itself" which "being so near Her Majesty's Palaces, it is and may be very dangerous to her Royal Person and government." Nothing much was done by "those in Power and Authority," though the Vatican instructed a handful of Jesuit priests to settle in Mayfair (now in the Church of the Immaculate Conception) and redeem the unredeemable. As the aristocracy moved into the nearby squares, the muggings and murders became intolerable and the fair was finally suppressed by George the Third.

Through the late 18th and early 19th centuries, PARK LANE (running along the side of Hyde Park) became a strand of great houses built and lived in by aristocrats with such names as Dorchester and Grosvenor. Although one or two fine Regency houses remain at the north end, the last of the ducal mansions were pulled down in the late 1920s and their owners are faintly remembered only in luxury hotels that bear their names. The great and near-great, the famous and fashionable who lived, entertained and frolicked in Mayfair would fill a tourist guidebook. Disraeli and Somerset Maugham wrote novels here, the Duke of Wellington philandered, Clive committed suicide, Winston Churchill set up house as a bridegroom and Tallulah Bankhead as a hellcat.

From the Civil Aviation Authority's compulsory minimum height of one thousand feet, a helicopter view can show little of the charm of many Georgian streets, the ancient pubs, the rambling alleys of mews and the elegance of many still-standing 18th century houses. But the geography of the streets is well defined. Cut up as a jigsaw puzzle, this page would tease the expertise and the nerve ends of the most knowledgeable Londoner.

In the 1880s, there was an architectural fashion for what became known as PONT STREET DUTCH, a domestic style in red brick with decorated gables that ran riot over Mayfair. One would have expected the English to build Dutch houses even cosier than the originals but, oddly, they enlarged the prototype into whole rows of five and six story houses (now broken into flats) that appear out of scale with the surrounding Georgian streets. The incongruous modern block (upper left) is the new Britannia hotel. The central garden is the MOUNT STREET GARDENS, and at the panhandle end of them the Jesuit CHURCH OF THE IMMACULATE CONCEPTION, where—it is said—Evelyn Waugh was converted to Rome.

Standing between the gardens and fronting on South Audley Street is GROSVENOR CHAPEL (1730) which during the Second World War became a special place of worship for the American armed forces.

(OPPOSITE) North from the edge of Grosvenor Square and a corner roof of the American Embassy (lower right) NORTH AUDLEY STREET runs through a forest of Pont Street Dutch up to Oxford Street and ends at the southwest corner of SELFRIDGE'S, with its long cliff of columns. Beyond is Baker Street running along the eastern edge of PORTMAN SQUARE, once a splendid square of Adam houses not built by the brothers. During the Second War it was bombed beyond redemption and now, except for one house (No. 20) built by Robert Adam, it is a melange of inept or clumsy modern.

Gordon Selfridge was a Chicagoan who astounded Londoners by setting up his "trade palace," the first English department store, in 1909. He was bristling with ingenuity: he exhibited Blériot's airplane one day after its pioneer flight across the Channel. He staged the first public show of television. He threw Lucullan election night parties for English society on the roof. He lived the life of Croesus and died a pauper.

GROSVENOR SQUARE is so called after Sir Richard Grosvenor, who laid it out in 1725 and whose estate came to own, and still does, large parcels of the most valuable land in London. The mistress of George the First was one of the square's first residents, and it at once became a fashionable place, if only a stone's throw from the rowdy sink of Mayfair.

For nearly two centuries it stood as one of the finest examples of Georgian domestic architecture. But very little remains, though the large blocks, now comprising offices or hotels, which enclose the east and south sides, have conformed to a regulation Georgian style. John Adams lived in the house at the extreme northeastern corner and started an American association that today encompasses the square in the shapes of the statue of President Franklin Roosevelt and the new American Embassy with its overriding gilt eagle. Eero Saarinen, who designed it, intended the eagle to have a wing-spread three times its present width. But the building itself, symbolizing to some Britons too brutal an intrusion by a superpower on the London domestic scene, caused enough of a rumpus. However, in the twenty years since it was built, so much stolid and dim "modern" architecture has proliferated in London that Saarinen's work begins to look to many natives graceful, even majestic.

During the Second World War, the Supreme Allied Commander had his headquarters here, and the square became known as Eisenhowerplatz.

(OPPOSITE) The most famous historical vestige of old Mayfair is the stone-faced mansion at Hyde Park Corner overshadowed now by a new hotel on an island in Piccadilly and by the towering London Hilton.

It is APSLEY HOUSE, the London home of the Duke of Wellington after he had beaten Napoleon, retired from the army and gone into politics. It was completed in 1778 by Robert Adam, and fifty years later the Duke added the Corinthian portico. It is now The Wellington Museum, a vivid and entertaining memoir of the Duke's life and times, with his swords, batons, decorations, orders, silver plate, porcelain, and a remarkable collection of paintings, some of them looted from the Spanish royal collections by Joseph Buonaparte and looted from him in turn by the Duke after the Battle of Vitoria in 1813.

Apsley House, the first building in Piccadilly, carries the awesome address: No. 1, London.

From the northern corner of Hyde Park, this view looks due west from MARBLE ARCH (right bottom corner) along BAYSWATER ROAD to the point where it turns into Notting Hill Gate. It is a stretch of town whose history has gone from the ghoulish, in the 12th century to the elegant, in the 19th.

Marble Arch, designed by Nash and here transplanted from its original site opposite Buckingham Palace, marks the northern end of Park Lane. Between it and the pond with three fountains is Tyburn Way, the spot where for six centuries famous criminals and martyrs were dragged from the Tower and executed on a triangular gallows. Today, the little curving cross street is a parking place for buses, since its incorporation in the rather awkward roundabout traffic plan led not to freedom and Oxford Street but to hopeless congestion.

Bayswater Road is for the most part still a street of graceful stucco houses and terraces put up, as a modest but fashionable challenge to Belgravia, between 1830 and 1860, before the Victorians had laid their heavy hand on domestic architecture. The story goes that it was "on the wrong side of the Park" to lure the grandees of Belgravia. But although today most of its houses have been converted into small hotels, it is still one of the most attractive residential parts of the city, and the value of its real estate, fronting on the Park, is staggering.

Behind the first terrace west of the Edgware Road, a clump of foliage is, alas, the only indication of CONNAUGHT SQUARE, one of the most handsome and secluded squares in London.

(OPPOSITE) Northwest of the city, beyond Wembley, is a hill that rises 200 feet above a surrounding plain of suburbia. It is called Harrow-on-the Hill. Here nestling below the sharp, dark spire of the parish church (in whose yard Byron's daughter Allegra lies in an unmarked grave) are the buildings, mostly Victorian, of the second most famous public (i.e. private) school in England: HARROW, due northeast about ten miles, and an architectural world away, from Eton. The number and nationalities of its famous pupils tease the imagination. Sheridan went here, and so did Byron, Palmerston, Trollope, Galsworthy, Pandit Nehru, King Faisal of Iraq, Hussein of Jordan, and Winston Churchill.

KENSAL GREEN CEMETERY, north and west of the city, and lying between the Harrow Road and the railroad tracks, is possibly the most extraordinary "congregation of the dead" in Europe.

Until well into the 19th century, the London dead were buried in open fields, which—as the grave stones were uprooted and piled along fences—turned into picnic grounds. The stench alone provoked a Royal Commission and the subsequent laying out of commercial public cemeteries. Kensal Green in 1833 was the first. It was given a touch of social prestige by the burial of two of George the Third's children, who were followed by Thackeray, both Brunels, Trollope and—as we now see—over 50,000 corpses of lesser fame.

HAMPSTEAD, a borough northwest of the city, was chartered as a "homestead" in the 10th century. Its HEATH is the largest and most jealously preserved of the Londoner's public parks. Its rolling sandy tract began to attract builders so early as the 1820s. But they were all resisted and, in 1871, finally put to rout by an act of parliament which handed over the whole 825 acres to the ownership of the metropolitan government.

It is the highest point in London and in 1588 served as the watchtower, or main link in a strand of bea-cons running to Romney Marsh, to warn of the landing of the Spanish Armada. Its wooded valleys and bare hills have been denied the usual English passion for fine landscaping, and it remains the favorite place, on summer weekends, for as many as 100,000 Londoners to wander and picnic.

Rising over a long meadow that slopes to a concert ground by a lake is KENWOOD HOUSE, a mansion by Robert Adam built for George the Third's Lord Chief Justice in 1767-9 and bequeathed to the nation in 1927. It has a fine collection of English and Dutch paintings and carefully wooded grounds in which Alexander Pope and, later, Samuel Johnson used to walk and ruminate.

(OPPOSITE) On a brilliant Bank Holiday it was possible from our helicopter to spot by the Ponds one of the two hideaway lawns—one for males, one for females—on which office workers and other escapists are allowed to sunbathe, in the nude if they are discreet and so disposed.

For longer than any other nation, the English of all classes resisted the habit of living in apartment houses (or, as they say, blocks of flats). Until the First World War, the vast majority of English couples thought of home as a house, however humble, with a back garden. It is a prejudice that helped them survive the German submarine blockade of the island in the First World War by turning all their gardens into vegetable patches.

(OPPOSITE) Here are two perfect examples of the national preference: two housing estates—a middle class one on a hill lying north and east of PARLIAMENT HILL FIELDS, which fringes the Highgate Ponds and Hampstead Heath; and a working class district, lying south and west of the Fields, that was built before the First World War.

On this estate, the houses that stand to the left of the long bisecting road and line the right side of it were built between the wars. But in the right foreground we see rows of small apartment houses built mostly after the Second War.

Even here, the English love of a gable is not abandoned but amplified in nine-story blocks of flats indulging a riot of neo-Tudor decoration.

# FESTIVALS

This imposing stadium, northwest of the city at WEMBLEY, was built for the 1924 British Empire Exhibition and ever since has been host to countless international athletic events (the Olympic Games of 1948 were held here). But its finest hour (and a half) comes on a Saturday afternoon in May, when the Football Association (soccer) Cup Final is played.

Here the partisan mobs are assembled for the 1979 final. The band is playing (OVERLEAF) as the Prince of Wales greets the two teams (Arsenal and Manchester United) before the kick-off.

In the once bosky but now heavily built-up district of St. John's Wood is the Vatican, or St. Andrews, of the game of cricket: LORDS cricket ground, which is owned by the Marylebone Cricket Club, the ruling body of the game since 1788.

It is named after Thomas Lord, who gave his name to a rude pitch in the middle of Dorset Square in 1787.

Twenty-seven years later, he transported the turf of the original to this site.

Beyond the cricket ground are the practice nets or "nursery", to the left of them the set-back terraces of the new Wellington Hospital, the most expensive private hospital in London, which has its signs in English, Arabic and German.

There was a time when the All-England Lawn Tennis Club's WIMBLEDON courts were surrounded by open meadows and a small enclosure for the nobs who owned automobiles. Today the area of the car parks is greater than that of "the action," and during the fortnight of the championship the cars desecrate the golf course in the adjoining Wimbledon Park.

(OPPOSITE) What, after a hundred years of the game, is there to say about WIMBLEDON that its fans do not already know? Here, on the Wednesday of the Women's semi-finals in 1979, Evonne Cawley (left) and Chris Evert Lloyd can be seen warming up on the No. 1 court. Two minutes later, play was due to start and our helicopter was told to vanish. (Mrs. Lloyd won 6-2, 6-3, but was demolished by Martina Navratilova in the final).

Far up river, beneath the wooded slope of the Chiltern hills, is Henley-on-Thames, where since 1839 the HENLEY REGATTA has taken place early in July. It is rowed over a course of one mile, 45 yards, in a narrow lane wide enough to allow only two shells to compete at a time. Here we see, upstream, two competing boats and the umpire's launch in their wake.

(RIGHT) The last stretch and the finishing post opposite the grandstand on the right bank. Below the large boat storage tent is the 1786 bridge and (lower left) the Henley parish church.

Seventy years ago, Baedeker called the Regatta "the Mecca of English boating men." Since then, it has become the supreme international rowing event, and the long British dominance of the sport has been defied and overthrown (as with golf and tennis) by such outlanders as Swedes, Americans and Russians. After 140 years as an exclusively male sport, the official word has gone out that in 1981 it will go co-educational.

The flat-racing season has two great events: the Derby, run at Epsom in early June; and later in the month ASCOT WEEK, run at Ascot Heath, which lies five miles southwest of Windsor. Here, on Gold Cup Day, the royal family is seen arriving in the grounds. The single horsemen are the master and huntsmen of the Royal Buckhounds.

(OPPOSITE) The royal procession winds through the gates of the enclosure as hundreds of ordinary people crowd against the fence, while in the enclosure itself the lucky and the rich stand with their ladies at their ease in their faded cutaways or, not at ease, in their rented ones.

# BY RIVER OUT OF THE CITY

No album of photographs, shot from above or below, could begin to do justice to the ROYAL BOTANICAL GARDENS AT KEW, which are beyond compare anywhere as a vast park, plant and flower nursery, herbarium (7 million dried plants), research institute, and training center for gardeners from all around the world. And no aerial photograph—especially when the summer foliage blankets the grounds—can encompass the range of flowers and trees, familiar and exotic, that blossom and bloom in spring and early summer.

It started in 1759 as a hobby of Princess Augusta, the mother of George the Third, and her head gardener.

As it grew, she commissioned little temples and the famous Pagoda (OVERLEAF), and John Nash designed a house for tropical plants. After her death, Sir Joseph Banks, who had been with Captain Cook on his first voyage around the world, dispatched gardeners to Africa, Asia and the Pacific islands to fetch home specimens of hundreds of plants. The Victorians, with typical thoroughness, set off to collect seeds and seedlings of every temperate and tropical flower and tree that took their fancy. Kew Gardens had taken the breadfruit tree to the West Indies, and in the second half of the 19th century introduced quinine to India and rubber to Malaysia. Glass houses abound. There is

a fine library; an Orangery, which exhibits the scientific and botanical work being done; a Palm House displaying every known variety of palm; a Water-Lily House, a house for desert plants, a laboratory for research on plant anatomy, a rock garden, a museum of general botany, and separate houses for alpine flowers, "stove plants", South African plants, orchids, etc etc etc.

But to the leisurely rambler through its 288 acres, it is a gardener's paradise, blazing with every flower and plant he has ever seen, read or dreamt about.

(OPPOSITE) Across from Kew Gardens on the north bank is a spacious park, and SYON HOUSE, for several centuries the home of the Dukes of Northumberland, for one of whom Robert Adam, in 1776, converted an old monastery into this graceful turreted house. Its gardens, its remarkable show of garden sculpture (OVERLEAF) especially, are not to be missed. But the interior of the house is the great thing, an elegant fantasia on the Adam style, from the design in black and white marble and stucco of the Grand Hall to the furniture and fireplaces.

South of the river, where it loops down between Barnes and Kew Bridge, lie the 2,350 unspoiled and undecorated acres of RICHMOND PARK, which like most other London parks was one time a royal preserve eventually passed on to the people. This one was enclosed by Charles the First. It is the only London park that is kept well-stocked with deer.

The house is WHITE LODGE, put up in 1729 for George the Second. It was the birthplace of King Edward the Eighth, whose brother lived here before he succeeded after the abdication. It is now the headquarters of the Royal Ballet School.

127

Richmond is luckier than most other parks in that its horizon is not defiled by power stations or high-rise concrete packing boxes but is decorated by the most elegant and harmonious housing estate to go up since the Second World War: at the eastern edge of the park, the ROEHAMPTON GARDEN ESTATE, which at first glance could well be mistaken for an extension of Hollywood's Century City.

This lavish sports ground, with its four cricket pitches, swimming pool, hard and grass tennis courts, and bowling green, is at Barnes. In the left corner is a reservoir hard by the Thames. The ground is enclosed by the curving Lonsdale Road and the grimly named Verdun Road, a late reminder of that battle of the First World War.

(OPPOSITE) HAMPTON COURT, the Tudor masterpiece of England, was built by Cardinal Wolsey, a ruthless statesman, wheeler-dealer, marriage-broker, real-estate genius, and a womanizer as catholic as Henry the Eighth himself. The Court, which contains a thousand apartments, was designed expressly for the Cardinal's own pleasure, but when he sensed (correctly) that his day was done, he reluctantly "presented it" to his King and master. More buildings and gardens were added to the original, most notably by Wren. The State Apartments are a treasure house of over 500 paintings, including the English portraitists Lely and Kneller, most of the Dutch masters, and a splendid profusion of the Italian school.

The extensive gardens of HAMPTON COURT, as we see them today, were laid out by William the Third, who incorporated in them a sunken garden and a tennis court built by Henry the Eighth. He added such oddities as a garden of aromatic herbs and a Great Vine, which annually yields over 500 bunches of Black Hamburgh grapes. In the extreme north corner of what amounts to a large meadow, and which William whimsically called 'The Wilderness', is his famous MAZE.

(OPPOSITE) Most of the water supply of London is drained from the rivers and streams that flow from the low chalk hills of the Thames Valley. Here, at SUNBURY, is the farthest point from the estuary at which water is taken (below Teddington weir, the river becomes tidal and mixes with sea water).

And here is a vivid reminder that it was the ancient Romans who invented what is to this day the fundamental working system whereby water is taken from the river, is pumped into RESERVOIRS, and sinks by gravity through coarse sand into FILTER BEDS (lower right-hand corner up through the center of the picture) where finer sand anchors tiny natural organisms that feed on floating bacteria and so help to purify the water.

What *we* have done since then, with increasing desperation since the flood tide of the Industrial Revolution, has been to use drastic mechanical and chemical devices to rid the river of the vast variety of pollutants that have already poured into it. In the 1960s, parliament was persuaded by the Thames Water Authority and the Port of London Authority to pass stiff legislation which requires oil, paper, sugar, detergent and other industries to purify their wastes. This dramatic discipline, exercised from the estuary to the limit of the tidal river, has been successful enough to encourage the return of bird species long unseen, and to prompt the TWA, in its last annual report, to contribute a startlingly hopeful note: "Salmon fry have been placed in three tributaries of the river to monitor their growth, dispersion and survival."

In a maze of tributaries and reservoirs west of Sunbury, is THORPE PARK, now being developed as a "leisure park": a river playground with racetrack, artificial beach, model airplanes and sports fields.

Twenty miles west of the city, east of Windsor and south of the M-4 motorway, is HEATHROW, one of the two or three busiest airports in the world. It replaced, in 1946, the first London air terminal, at Croydon, which started the world's first regular commercial passenger flights in 1919.

Here is an airport as the incoming pilot sees it. This dramatic picture was a lucky shot taken in a hurry, for the British Civil Aviation Authority is as strict as any there is. It bans all private airplanes here and does not take kindly to a hovering helicopter.

About six miles north of Heathrow as the jets fly, and ten miles north of the river (but not to be excluded on a technicality) is PINEWOOD, which claims to be the largest movie studio in Europe. Certainly, it must be unrivaled for its technical resources, as anyone can testify who has seen James Bond fight submarines and freighters inside these enormous rooms.

The bare ground in which the big white sound stage is planted was once a Roman city, glistening with columns and rialtos, constructed for the Elizabeth Taylor epic, *Cleopatra*. But when Miss Taylor languished through a serious illness, the studio adopted the ingenious idea of filming the Roman epic in Rome.

No doubt the sudden glimpse of that white building and its ominous label—007—was what hypnotized us into taking this shot.

135

Between Staines and Windsor lies this great meadow of RUNNYMEDE and (OPPOSITE) MAGNA CARTA IS-
LAND: preserved for the nation as the spot where King
John was compelled by his barons to sign the first charter
of English liberty. The entrance gates and lodges were designed by Sir Edwin Lutyens.

Above Runnymede and commanding a splendid view of it from COOPER'S HILL is this graceful cloistered house, which was dedicated in 1953 as a memorial to the more than 20,000 men and women of the COMMONWEALTH AIR FORCES who lost their lives in the Second World War and have no known graves.

(OPPOSITE) William The Conqueror, the archetype of the warrior king, built WINDSOR CASTLE, his royal residence, on this chalk hill, which commands a long view of the river valley, and of any approaching enemy. His original has long vanished, but from Henry the Third, in the 13th century, to Victoria, at the end of the 19th, many monarchs have built, rebuilt, extended, altered or restored everything from mediaeval dungeons, and a Gothic cathedral (the splendid St. George's chapel, left of the Round Tower), to royal apartments which are Tudor or Gothic on the outside, Georgian on the inside.

If this vast collection of towers, battlements, chapels and houses has any unity at all, it is due to Sir Jeffrey Wyatville, an early 19th century Gothic revivalist, who was commissioned by George the Fourth to transform the whole scene. Wyatville did so under the impulse most stingingly expressed by a pupil architect —Augustus Pugin—in a pamphlet denouncing Georgian and Regency architecture for being "degraded" and urging a general restoration of "the Christian style."

(OPPOSITE) WINDSOR CASTLE is one mile in circumference and adjoins the so-called Home Park of over 400 acres.

Deep in the woods that ring the south boundary of Windsor Great Park is VIRGINIA WATER, an artificial lake created by the Duke of Cumberland who was the conquerer of Bonnie Prince Charlie.

Adjoining the rolling woods of Virginia Water and running south-southwest for several miles is a geological sliver of sand and pine country, heathland ideal for links golfers far from the sea. Here is a famous course, fringed by prosperous country and suburban houses that have earned this neighborhood the title of the Stockbroker Belt.

This is SUNNINGDALE, the favorite playground of the former King Edward the Eighth but more distingished still as the course on which the immortal Robert Tyre (Bobby) Jones, Jr. established a course record (66). One of the clubs that helped him do it is reverently mounted over the mantlepiece in the clubhouse.

(OPPOSITE) ETON COLLEGE, one of the most ancient and famous of English public (i.e. private) schools, stands appropriately in the patrician shadow of Windsor Castle. Henry the Sixth put up the first buildings, which still stand, between 1440 and 1490, as a foundation for a provost, 10 priests, 6 choristers, one schoolmaster, and 25 "poor scholars."

These provisions have been —shall we say?—relaxed down the centuries, during which Eton became the preserve, both social and scholarly, of the upper classes and of succeeding generations of merchants who aspired to upper-classdom. Whether or not Eton has produced, as the saying goes, "the best and the worst of England," it has without question contributed a large proportion of the oarsmen in the annual Oxford and Cambridge boat race and, until very recently, a strikingly disproportionate number of ministers in British Cabinets.

(OPPOSITE) This comic, almost Disneyland, model of a fortress complete with battlements and cannon balls, is FORT BELVEDERE, on the edge of Windsor Great Park.

When, in 1928, King George the Fifth was seriously ill, the Prince of Wales—who had had a couple of dangerous spills in point-to-point races —was persuaded by his mother to give up steeple-chasing. He sold his horses and looked around for a week-end retreat somewhere in the golfer's "pine and sand" paradise southwest of the city. He found it in this run-down, old 18th century, rebuilt folly, a so-called "Grace and Favor" house, one which is at the disposal of the Royal family and is usually given to widows and pensioners.

Here, as Prince of Wales, he found a haven of privacy for his Anglo-American social set. Here, as King, he found an uneasy refuge from the heartache of the scandal that attached to his affair with Mrs. Simpson. And here, on the 10th of December 1936, he sat down in the drawing room that looks out to the woods, and signed the following Instrument of Abdication:

"I, Edward the Eighth, of Great Britain, Ireland and the British Dominions beyond the seas, King, Emperor of India, do hereby declare my irrevocable determination to re-nounce the throne for myself and for my descendants and my desire that effect should be given to this instrument of ab-dication immediately."

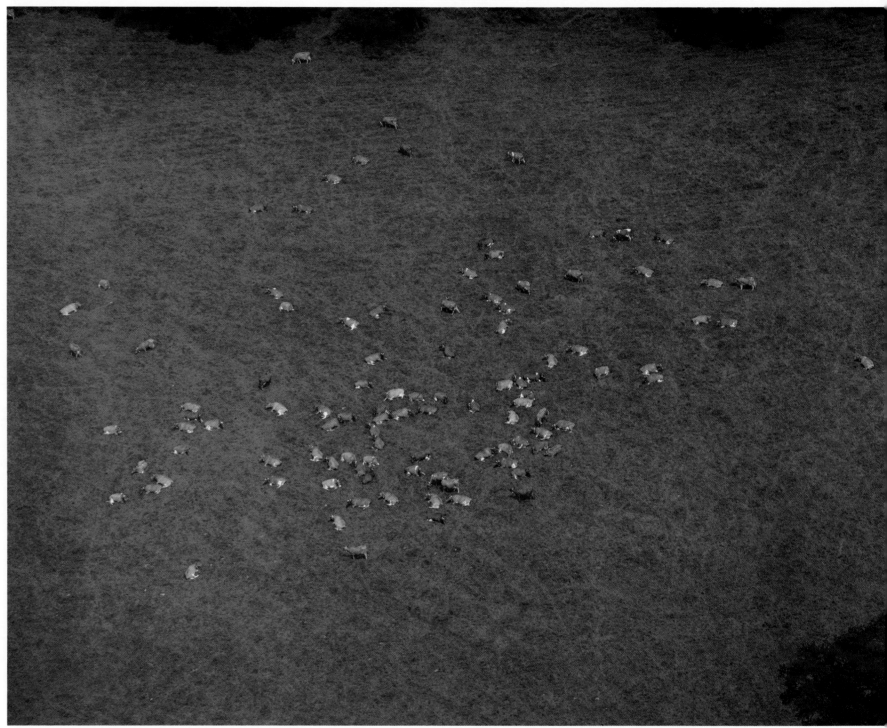

While the Queen enjoys the racing at ASCOT, her prize herd of Guernsey cattle snooze in the noonday sun in an adjoining meadow.

145

BRAY, about 25 miles upriver, was once a way station for the river traffic in malt, mead and timber. Today it does a brisk summertime business with boating parties, anglers and week-end lovers of pleasure. The church (upper left), with a battlemented square tower, is mostly 13th century. It is generally believed to be that of the Vicar of Bray, except by Irishmen, who claim both the song and its hero. In the right-hand lower corner is Jesus Hospital, founded in 1627, and its alms-houses for 26 people, who must be over fifty to live there.

Between Bray and Taplow, this bridge at AMERDEN PONDS is said to be the first railroad bridge across the Thames.

CLIVEDEN, just north of Taplow, has been famous in our time as the country seat of the Astors, and famous at all times for its magnificent beech woods and garden. The 17th century original burned down, and so did its replacement. The present mansion dates from 1849.

The gardens were given to the National Trust in 1942. The house stayed in the family until the death of second Viscount Astor in 1966, but, in accordance with his wish that it be used to further understanding between the English-speaking peoples, it was eventually leased by the Trust to Stanford University, California, as one of its overseas branches.

During the 1930s, it got a bad name among leftists and liberals in England as a sort of Conservative hatchery for appeasement of Hitler, even though many of its regular guests were politicians, both Conservative and Labor, who were staunchly opposed to Prime Minister Neville Chamberlain and his followers. Yet, during the year before the outbreak of the Second War, Harold Nicolson bemoaned the mischief that "the Cliveden set" was likely to do abroad: "In the last resort," he wrote in his diary, "our decision is embodied, not in Mayfair or in Cliveden, but in the provinces. The harm which these silly, selfish hostesses do is immense. They convey to foreign envoys the impression that policy is decided in their own drawing rooms."

(OPPOSITE) The rear or courtyard view reveals Cliveden's superb location by the river.

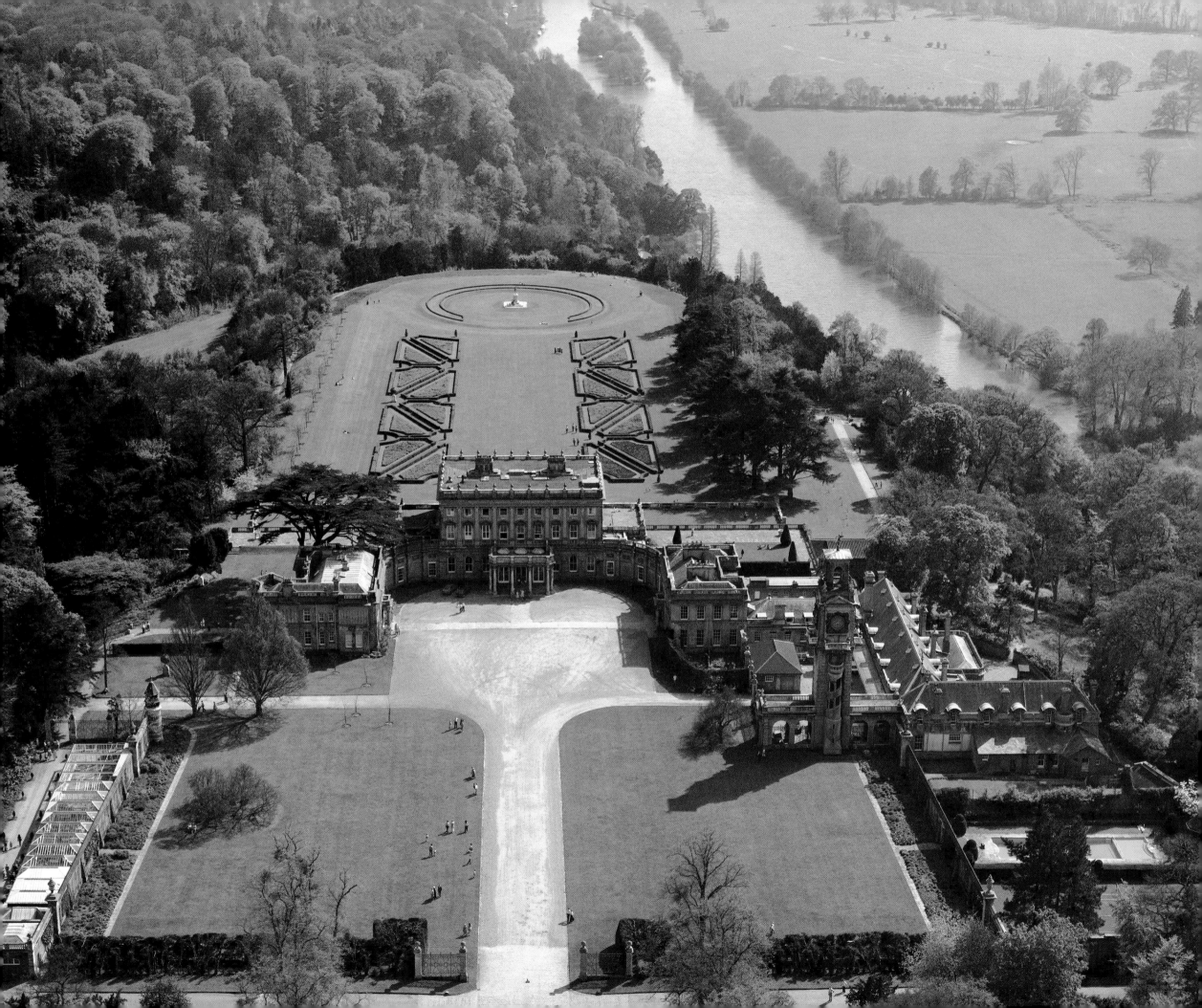

Winding north past Maidenhead, the river flows
into spreading meadowland over which (the Civil Aviation Authority's map warns) there is "Intense Gliding
Activity." COOKHAM Weir is at the bottom right and,
just over the trees, the main navigation channel. Here,
and in all its pleasant creeks, are plentiful perch, pike
and roach.

(OPPOSITE) MARLOW, a fishing station since the time
of Elizabeth the First, retains—from the air at any rate—a
pleasing Tudor quality, if you don't look close enough to
see that the "Tudor" gabled bungalows were built mainly
before and after the First World War and are an overlay
on what was essentially a Georgian town. In the church
to the left of the graceful little suspension bridge is the
tomb of Sir Miles Hobart, a Roundhead who has the distinction of having had the first monument put up in England at the public expense.

(OPPOSITE) Shelley lived in MARLOW and wrote much of *The Revolt of Islam* while boating along this stretch of the river.

Close by the lock and weir is an original bit of river housing—white weather-boarding and tilted rooflines—by Seymour Harris.

In seventy years, while the population of the United States has more than doubled, the population of the United Kingdom has increased by only 25%. But England, Scotland, Wales and Northern Ireland together comprise an area smaller than Oregon, and the population density is ten times that of the United States.

Inevitably, housing is a chronic problem and, after a period of conflict between rural councils and people fleeing from the cities, mobile home communities (known in Britain as "caravan parks") came to be licensed. Here is one just above Marlow but fenced off from the nearby village and from the river people by hedges of shade trees.

From the air, an American might well mistake this for a shot of Kansas: a homesteader's "section" (i.e. a square mile of land). It is, however, a stretch of grassland between Henley and High Wycombe and an ideal launching ground for a toy blimp.

(OPPOSITE) There are 44 locks and weirs in the Thames system. This one, Hambledon Lock, downstream from Henley, was the last one we filmed. Beyond it, the river finally escapes from the suburbs into the uplands and farming country of the Thames Valley.

(OPPOSITE) A storm approaching from the west highlights the undulations of the THAMES VALLEY and sets off both the limitations and the charm of much English farming: a one-man business requiring the fencing in of separate small holdings, of crops, pasture and grazing land with neat hedges and woods. Looking out on such a landscape from a nearby hill, Mark Twain remarked: "The English countryside is too beautiful to be left outdoors; it ought to be put under glass."

A twilight glimpse of the upper river—"the stream of pleasure"—as it moves north and west far from the city into the placid farmland of Oxfordshire.

A NOTE OF THANKS

Apart from the visible dedication of Jane Olaug Kristiansen, who designed the whole book, and Ken Leong and Suzanne Lawlor, who proofread the text, there are many Londoners, native and adopted, not to mention several exiled Scots, who took an affectionate interest in this project from the start and helped us either with the logistics or with suggestions and reminders along the way

We are particularly grateful to John Warner, of Air Film Services Ltd.; to Chris Hunt, Chris Powell and Tony Dando of British Caledonian Helicopters; to Joan Pollard and Colin Sorensen of the Museum of London; to John Wilson, John Saville and Michael Tunnicliffe of New Scotland Yard; to Stan Jones and A.G. Mackie of the Civil Aviation Authority; to Roy Johnson of the Port of London Authority; to Laurie Moles and John Smith of the Thames Water Authority; and to a raft of friends that include Hatsuro Aizawa, Bill Stroh, Ann Turner, Russell Paige, Alan Owen, Sir Iain Stewart, John Stanley, Ray Dunnett and John Calmann. Of course, errors and omissions are not to be ascribed to any of them.

I should also like to say that amid the mass of literature on the subject, from Nikolaus Pevsner to the *Dictionary of National Biography*, two works stand out as invaluable to the wanderer around London whether he is on the ground or in the air. David Piper's *Companion Guide to London* is incomparably entertaining, and of all the regular guidebooks, the *Blue Guide* seems to me to be the most alert and informative.

A. C.

The text of this book is set in a typeface known as ITC Garamond Light, a 1976 design by Tony Stan, based on letter forms originally created by a Parisian, Claude Garamond (1480?–1561), a pupil of Geoffrey Tory, the popularizer of the French Renaissance style of book decoration. With Tory's encouragement, Garamond developed roman typefaces of such grace and clarity that they eventually ousted gothic letters from European typography outside Germany.